Alana's Advice...
When There's a Clique,
You've Got to Think Quick

By Alexandra Sabina Bender

Crown House Publishing Limited
www.Crownhousepublishing.com
www.crownhouse.co.uk

Published by

Crown House Publishing Company, LLC
6 Trowbridge Drive, Suite 5, Bethel, CT. 06801
www.crownhousepublishing.com

and

Crown House Publishing Ltd
Crown Buildings
Bancyfelin, Carmarthen, Wales SA33 5ND, UK
www.crownhouse.co.uk

For further information about the
Teacher's Study Guide for this title,
please contact info@chpus.com.

13 Digit ISBN: 978-1845900755

LCCN: 2007926617

Manufactured in the United States of America

Dedication

This book is dedicated to....

My Family: My awesome parents, sister and aunt. You'll find some traits in the characters were inspired by you.

My Friends: The coolest girls and guys ever. Good traits from you will be found in here. The people from my school, to my town in Connecticut, and the rest of the world (three heartbeats away), you'll always be remembered.

Contents

Introduction

I wrote this because I wanted everyone to get the message that it is okay to be different and unique. Unfortunately in middle and high school, kids often divide themselves up into various cliques that are based on a similar (if not the same) type of personality.

Sometimes bullying happens in or out of school because kids see others as threats because they are "different," "weird," "nerdy," or just because of problems at home. However, people are different in many ways. The differences are not always tolerated and one group will deliberately exclude kids that are not the same as other clique members. Sometimes they can be very controlling as well.

One group or one person should not be allowed to have the power to control who you can like, what, or who is cool or not, or what you do. Do you really want someone else deciding these things for you? Is being popular really worth what it might cost in the end? Don't you want to be different and if nothing else, do the things you like to do? Wouldn't you rather have real friends than just be part of a clique where everyone blindly follows some ring leader? What are you willing to "pay" for?

We don't have to be enemies. People who have tempers can learn from people who are calm. People who are dyslexic can learn to learn to write in different ways. We all can improve by learning from each other but especially from those that are different. We do not have to "hate" every (or any) little flaw that someone else might have. Hate is a very dangerous emotion. We have seen for too long the bad consequences of exclusion in adults: elitism, prejudice, and discrimination.

Nobody has to or should hate anyone at all. Unfortunately, many (even adults) choose to act this way and when societies choose to turn against each other because of differences, it results in war. There is always the option of taking the higher road, which in the long run, can only lead to a higher society.

Two of the characters in this book, Alana and Jane, are enemies and they choose to despise each other. The two girls do not understand each other because they do not really know the details about each other's lives. Alana, in most instances, tries to be the better person and just walk away from confrontations. Jane, on the other hand, acts out, but neither of them is perfect. But fate has a way of changing things in a most unexpected way.

Some people are happy, while others are not, but the forced facades of school make it hard to tell who is really feeling what about anything.

Understanding and tolerating diversity be it cultural, economic, social or personality differences is a major issue with both kids and adults starting as early as elementary school. People feel a need for whatever reasons they may have to claim that they are better, smarter, or more talented than others. There is always another way. Little flaws should be worked around somehow. It is not a good idea to act bigheaded, and sometimes a really nagging flaw is hard to swallow, but that doesn't mean you have to hate someone. People can't help their habits. Tolerance is the key.

Sometimes if someone tries to act like the bigger person and apologize, it is not accepted. There is no problem between two people large enough to merit fighting or holding a grudge for a long time. When someone says those two powerful little words to you, "I'm sorry," try to accept them, forgive them, *and move on.* It is not up to one person—it is up to everyone.

Words and actions do have consequences. Call me weird, or call me crazy and maybe I don't care, but then again, I just might. If we can understand how to live together as kids in school, perhaps we can also do the same as adults in society.

Alexandra Sabina Bender

The Beginning

Dear Alana,

I'm nervous about the end of school. Things will change and I will have to move to another school where I hear one large clique is downright nasty. I need help on how to survive. How do I not end up like a loner? -Not A Loner

Dear Loner,

Change is inevitable (can't be avoided). It's completely natural to be nervous about a new school. Try to not be rude to the clique, but don't suck up to them either. To make friends find someone who shares a few of the same interests as you. If you stick up for yourself in tough situations and don't give in to the reaction that others try to provoke; they will back off. -Alana ☺

"Class pay attention," cried Ms. Limner. "The history final will be in a week and not many of you are prepared."

Ms. Limner, a long time teacher of seventh grade at James Walk Middle School, liked to make sure "to the letter" that everyone in the class knew the material. She always told her students that no one would ever fail even a practice test, which she gave every week. Rumors flew that Ms. Limner spent too much time on work which is why everyone felt that her once beautifully long red hair grayed out early.

"Do you hear me everyone? Jackie, Alana?"

"We hear you loud and clear," they replied in unison, but secretly, Jackie Donner and Alana Shannonson had been busy discussing plans for their long weekend, something they did quite often. Since it was Thursday in the summery month of June, every student was worked up, excited, and rapidly losing interest in school.

"Now I want everyone studying hard or they will find themselves in summer school," Ms. Limner said with a glare in Jackie and Alana's direction. "Class dismissed!" A bell chimed a minute later. It was the end of a very tedious school day and Alana and Jackie were now on their way to the classroom where the newspaper committee met.

*   *   *

"Alana, you are unusually quiet. You almost always are looking forward to answering letters for the advice column that you edit in the Walk Street Journal, our school news-paper," Jackie pointed out. "What's up? There's a long week-end starting tomorrow and you haven't been on "IM" lately. Plus you are always full of ideas and there's not a single scheme brewing in that overlarge brain at all. Are you on a blank or something?"

"Huh, Oh I.... um....have something on my mind," Alana responded blankly as she stared at the computer screen which had a page that read *Ask Candy Apple! Inquire what you desire!*

Although her advice name was Candy Apple, everyone knew it was Alana who gave the advice so nobody paid the other name much attention anyway.

"Oh I see," Jackie said as she took a second look at the person near the classroom door. "Well, if it isn't 'the devil in cosmetics.' Am I correct?"

Jane Luklit, the editor-in-chief of the school newspa-per, The Walk Street Journal, (and the only real source of information at James Walk Middle School) stood at the door with a smirk on her face. She was talking with a fairly tall, blond-haired boy. Jane had a reputation at school for being a flirt as well as thinking she was all "that." She always wore too much of some sort of cheap makeup and a lot of perfume. Every room that Jane was in or near had a stench of chemicals. (Sometimes the chemical garb Jane wore made Alana feel that she wouldn't be able to breathe while next to her.) Also Jane was practically famous school-wide for being a gossip queen and naturally she had joined the newspaper committee.

Alana and Jackie, as well as many other girls, thought Jane was just there to annoy them. Thus her nickname to Alana and Jackie was "the devil in cosmetics" after their favorite book, *The Devil Wears Prada*. Jackie sometimes joked about how Jane was the bad side of Alana because they both had blue eyes, long light-brown hair and had a similar taste in activities, sports and clothes. It was impossible for Jackie and Alana to avoid her without getting dissed on almost everything. Jackie looked nothing like Jane. Jackie was blonde, had dark brown eyes and always wore a stylishly patterned hat or bandana. Needless to say, Alana and Jackie didn't get along at all with Jane. Their attitudes about everything almost always clashed.

Yet, there was one special thing that really distinguished Alana from Jane. That was Alana's lucky necklace. Alana wore a chained necklace with a jade stone that her archaeologist grandfather gave her before he died. Alana's grandfather found and polished the stone himself while on an expedition. This necklace was a comfort to Alana and helped her with her advice column so she never took it off. However, little did Alana know that the necklace would soon prove to be much more than just a pretty piece of jewelry.

"Why *hello*," said Jane with a big, fake smile to Alana and Jackie, "We have to get working now don't we? So enough chatting to each other, we have a deadline to meet."

"Well if work is so important, why aren't *you* doing anything at all?" exclaimed Alana with an icy glare.

"I am editor-in-chief," Jane said loudly making sure everyone near could hear. Nobody paid much attention. Everyone knew Jane expected to be noticed; she thought other kids should be impressed with her high rank. "I have to make sure that everyone, even the least important contributors have their articles in our paper on time so at least they have some chance at being read. If you'll excuse me I need to do *my* job. After all important people are never finished." Jane left to go work with the boy with whom she had been talking. She swung her light-brown hair and strutted over to his computer, and on her way she turned

7

to a younger girl, "Work on your enthusiasm, so the news in your article isn't so blah."

"It's fine. There's nothing wrong with any of the articles," the girl stated somewhat meekly. "That's what you think," said Jane as she kept walking.

"I see why you haven't been talking much today," smirked Jackie to Alana who tried her best to remain calm. "I'll remind you as we leave," she teased.

*   *   *

After the usual hour and a half of working on their articles, Alana and Jackie left school and started walking to Alana's house which wasn't far. They neared the Arben Harbor where a fairly large boat was docked proudly.

"Come on you know why you weren't talking much. Admit it," Jackie coaxed.

"Oh look, there's Captain Arben" Alana suddenly ran to the ship named *Treasure Hunter* where there stood a tall, bearded muscular man in a white shirt with an anchor on the pocket and white pants. He was polishing some sort of rock that he found on one of the islands he visited during a recent voyage. Alana's dad knew many people in the state of Connecticut and was a friend of Captain Arben. Alana's Dad sometimes sailed to various places in the state on weekends with the Captain but he didn't know Alana as well.

"Jackie, just to warn you, whispered Alana said. "My Dad says that Captain Arben always wanted to be a pirate in plays and movies, but since it would interfere with his golf game too much he never did. He just likes to talk like one, though."

"Ahoy, Ms. Alana how's yer dad doing?" Captain Arben boomed out in a gruff deep voice.

"He's fine and what did you find on the last voyage?" She eyed the objects in Captain Arben's hand.

"I found thing's ye'd never dream of."

"Did you find another galleon?"

"No, better than mere money, it's a stamp worth more than $20,000 from an important letter and this special

8

quartz crystal with gold and silver imbedded inside."

"Are you going to sell anything this time?"

"The stamp I'm a sellin'. The rock I'm a keepin'."

"Another addition to your collection. Well I hope you get what the stamp's worth. I have to go now."

As Alana turned to leave with Jackie, who had been admiring the ship with all its space, Captain Arben said,

"Yer in der school newspaper, am I correct?"

"She's the advice columnist," answered Jackie. Alana rubbed her necklace. The beautiful stone felt smooth in her fingers.

"That's what I thought, ya know me son, Chris?"

"Yes, I do," replied Alana.

"Well he wants ter take some of his girlfriends from school with him while we're on a voyage ter Boston this weekend fer a convention. Unfortunately he can only take along two first mates, and he wants ta know who ta choose. Chris wants ter make der right choice ya know."

"Well my mind is drawing a blank right now because of school and things but I will let you know tomorrow or as soon as I can." Alana replied.

"Take yer time. Sometimes I think yer a lot like yer old man, Ms. Alana. Ya take yer time and always end up with an answer. I'm a gonna hoist the Jolly Roger permanently and make ye walk der plank if ye say dat it ain't true." Alana and Jackie kept walking.

What did he mean by that? Hoist the Jolly Roger permanently? Alana wondered to herself. It would take a long time to find out.

At Home

Dear Alana,
    I have an extremely nosey relative who always asks for my most personal secrets. I never want to tell, but my relative will pry and poke until I give her the answer. My parents told her to stop doing this but she never listens. I always make up an excuse to get away from the subject but that doesn't work anymore What do I do?. -Needs privacy NOW

Dear Needs Privacy,
    Try telling your relative yourself to stop it instead of having your parents stick up for you all of the time. She might actually listen to you because it comes from you directly. Or, if that doesn't work, say that you have nothing to say and no secrets to share. There's nothing to ask for if there's no response. -Alana ☺

"Alana you can't hide it from me forever or even at all. You know what I want to say. I'm staying all night, and remember I *will* get it out of you." Jackie finally managed to corner Alana in her room after a half hour of running around outside.

"No I don't."

"You know one of the main reasons why you despise Jane..."

"Well, duh, she's a pain."

"And you..."

"Don't say it Jackie!"

"Like...maybe it's because of ..."

"I mean it Jackie!"

"Sean Pedene!"

"Grrrrr, you got it."

At James Walk Middle School, there were all kinds of cliques and gangs. The sporty guys and girls were considered popular, while writers and artists were below average on the 'in-crowd scale.' Jackie and Alana had known each other for years and Jackie knew that Alana wasn't big on the idea of popularity measures at school. Because Sean wasn't an idiot and was very creative in writing, and had a successful column as a news specialist, Alana had developed a crush on him. Jackie was the only person who knew this, but Alana had a suspicion that Jane was clued in to everything she felt.

"But why were you mad?" Jackie continued, "I knew something was up. You normally have ideas by the truckload. Today you are blanker than the blackboard in Gym class! Why is that?"

"Jane is a big flirt and Sean has fallen for the act. I've known him since first grade and we've been great friends forever, even if he doesn't speak to me as often as he does to Jane. Besides I see him everywhere and when that happens I can't get anything out of my head. Jane Luklit hasn't even known him for a year. Didn't you see them today working on the lead articles. Always talking, always working together, it's a pain. I can't even think straight. That's why I'm a blank."

"Why don't we listen to our favorite pop band, *The Planettes*, or watch our favorite show *Cow Daze* or look at the work you did before Sean moved to this part of town at the beginning of the year. Come on, what do you want to do first?" Coaxed Jackie holding up a poster of a group of teens in cow-skin boots along with a CD case of *The Planettes* which included a brunette, (Vanessa Venus,) a blonde, (Natasha Neptune) and a redhead (Missy Mercury) in futuristic silver outfits and jewelry with colors that matched their personality/planet.

(Alana never understood why film directors, writers and other creative types always thought that people in the future would be wearing identical silvery body suits for clothing.)

"Music," They said together smiling as if it was decided long ago.

12

So for an hour or more Alana and Jackie listened to *The Planettes*. They were even singing along to their favorite song, Solarverse.

Get up off your feet
The world needs you
You will also need the world
Because there are many things to meet

You have the unlimited power
You are always in control
Throw your curse back in reverse
And you'll be in solarverse

Nothing can keep you down long
If you have the proper mind
Be positive and smart and yourself
For confidence just sing this song

You have the unlimited power
You are always in control
Throw your curse back in reverse
And you'll be in solarverse

You'll always have your own strengths
Nobody can deny it
So Get up Get up Get Get Get up
You are on your way kid

You have the unlimited power
You are always in control
Throw your curse back in reverse
And you'll be in solarverse

You'll always have the unlimited power
You are always in control
Throw your curse back in reverse
And you'll be in solarverse

"Think of *The Planettes* song, "Lucky Charm," it suits you perfectly," Jackie added. She switched to the track.

It helps…It revives
And it's always by my side
I will know it's true
Some will find it sooner
But that doesn't mean
That you will never be in tune

You will find your lucky charm
It will help you with its confidence arm
You never know when you'll find your four-leaf
        clover
Take it before your good-dream is over

It can be anything in the whole wide world
A jewel, a book, or your home girl
Even if you don't realize
One day it will all be revealed

You will find your lucky charm
It will help you with its confidence arm
You never know when you'll find your four-leaf
        clover
Take it before your good-dream is over

You don't have to go down under
Let it free and out from wonder
It should rise higher than allowed
You should know that by now

You will find your lucky charm
It will help you with its confidence arm
You never know when you'll find your four-leaf
        clover
Take it before your good-dream is over

"Wow, you know the cure, Dr. Donner," Alana said. "Why aren't we writing together on the advice column."

"Because you are the one with the ideas and good luck charm and Jane won't let us work together because there is always "too much chatter.""

Alana touched her necklace's stone. "That jerk can be a real pest, snob and..."

"Hold it! You aren't the only one with problems, Alana. Even Misty from *Cow Daze* and the stage crew for *The Planettes* might have guy and girl trouble. Even the goddesses from your story last year had guy/god trouble! Everyone needs help sometimes and love lives aren't the only problems, you know. You do want to be a professional advice columnist don't you? Remember when we were in elementary school and we would laugh a lot because we didn't care about what anyone thought? Go back to that age and feeling!"

"I guess so," Alana yawned but she wasn't completely convinced.

Soon both girls were fast asleep. Alana always kept her necklace on when she slept and more often than not, falling asleep holding the stone in her hand.

The Harbor

Dear Alana,

    My friend keeps breaking into my locker, even with my lock on. He never takes anything but he leaves the most demented notes. I haven't told him to stop because he might threaten to spread around my combination and actually take things. Please don't say report him to my teacher or the principal because he WILL find out. -Victim

Dear Victim,

    You can try reporting the truth anonymously. Or why not just change your locker and/or your lock? If you tell your parents what is going on, I am sure they will buy a new lock. This time, don't tell anyone your combination. -Alana ☺

Alana suddenly woke up. She had overslept.

She and Jackie had to be at the harbor near the *Treasure Hunter*. When they got there they saw Chris Arben on the ship's deck surrounded by six girls wearing a feminine version of his uniform. The girls wore white short sleeved shirts with a gold anchor on the pocket, white skirts with pearls around their waists, and matching shoes with long blue silk ribbons (obviously done by the girls themselves) except for one. One girl even wore a hat. A blonde wore a gold anchored necklace. One brunette girl even wore gloves to prevent rope burn. It was hard to see who was who in the mass of white. Some girls were begging, others were bouncing, as they all of course wanted to go on the voyage, but it was obviously impossible as all six girls would never have fit on the fairly small ship. The back deck wasn't exactly the size of a ballroom.

"Hey Alana, hey Jackie," called Chris through the swarm. His tanned face and sandy colored hair gave some color to the blinding white.

"Where's your dad?" asked Alana.

"He's in the back of the ship waiting for me to make up my mind as to who I can bring, which is hard for me to do any time but especially now."

"I think you should choose someone who knows a lot about the water and ships and who isn't doing this just to impress you. Someone who is willing to put time and effort into the mission and knows what lies ahead. If you find two people who meet these standards you will know who to choose."

"Great advice Alana, thanks."

"OK," Chris turned to the girls and said, "Please form a line and take a step back if you agree with what I say. I can then choose who I will take." As the girls formed a line, looking a bit worried. Chris continued, "If you don't know anything about the ocean, please take one step back." Two girls stepped back, disappointed.

"If you don't know anything about ships, please take one step back." The girl with the hat grumbled as she reluctantly stepped back.

"Last statement. If you are using this trip as an excuse to get away for any reason please take one step back." Nobody stepped back this time.

"OK, the real final statement. If you normally have a busy schedule and know something might come up, and then you won't be able to come on the trip, please take one step back now," he finished as the girl with the white laces stepped back.

The girls that remained were Chrissie Rhodes, the blonde with the gold necklace, and Kim Cornnis, the brunette with the gloves.

"Who knew that Chrissie and Kim knew a lot about ships?" whispered Jackie. "But it would explain what they wear when they go to school and they're not that much younger than Chris."

Chrissie and Kim were thanking Chris endlessly as the sailor and sailorettes boarded the *Treasure Hunter*. Captain Arben boarded last and the ship sailed out. Alana thought she saw Captain Arben wink before the ship had left for Boston.

Goddess Gracious

Dear Alana,

I like this one person I see in many of my classes but they never talk to me. They look at me with kind of a smile. They never talk as much as they used to. This person is always with friends and I try to be as nice as possible. Do you have any hints on how I can get more attention?-Wallflower

Dear Wallflower,

Put your suspicions to the test and smile when this person looks at you. If it's a truly happy smile then you are good to go. You have to be sure it's you that this person sees when you flirt. On the other hand, if you get a polite smile or the person frowns and looks away it's a bad sign that they aren't too interested. -Alana ☺

As Alana and Jackie approached their favorite, secret place, a lovely, grassy area near Alana's house, they lay down. Daydreaming, they all of a sudden felt themselves floating gracefully upwards.

"Wow! I feel like I'm in one of your stories or one of my younger cousins books," exclaimed Jackie.

"If this is like one of my stories then this will lead us to the glittering cloud where the gods and goddesses of witches and wizards live," answered Alana. "If this is one of your cousin's books it will lead us to where good fairies and evil leprechauns live. It still was my idea to get there by floating and getting dropped on a cloud that bounces."

"Which just happened right now. How ironic," exclaimed Jackie.

"Definitely my story."

"How can you tell?"

"Look over there!" Alana pointed to a disappointed look-ing goddess hovering near a very large gold palace. She had faded red hair, and on her forehead was a pattern of rubies.. The pattern matched the rubies around her neck. She wore a cherry red robe that shined like a cloud, and had the same ruby pattern around the waist.

"Are we dreaming?" asked Jackie. She pinched herself, still awake. " I Doubt it."

The goddess stood up and the rubies glowed for a mo-ment. "Hello, what brings you here?" She spoke with a slightly timid tone.

"Hi. I'm Alana Shannonson and this is Jackie Donner. We somehow floated up here. You look sad. Is anything wrong?"

"I'm Miranda Mercury and I am disappointed because the god I love already has a girlfriend."

"Welcome to my world," muttered Alana.

"You don't know that for a fact," whispered Jackie. She swung Alana's lucky necklace from around her neck.

Alana turned to Miranda "There must be another god other than...who is it you like?"

Miranda stared down, "His name is Toronis Cupid. His girlfriend is Lexana Venus. Perhaps you know their grand-parents, Cupid and Venus, god and goddess of love. They are the grandchildren of the gods your ancestors knew."

"Well we don't know them personally, but we have heard of them," exclaimed Jackie. "We might help you find true love, but it wouldn't be with Toronis. What are you goddess of?"

"I am the goddess of messages and errands but the mes-senger god is always running errands continuously."

"What do you find lovable or attractive in a god or mor-tal?" Asked Alana.

"I prefer a god with smarts as well as sweetness, and someone who is strong as well. I also want someone who shares my interests. Finally, I also wouldn't mind someone who likes the color red."

"What about Mars?" suggested Jackie.

"Do you mean Moe Mars?" Miranda asked.

"Uh…Sure."

"Why don't you go look for him?" suggested Alana.

"He's the one in red robes and has brown-red hair standing just inside the golden gate doorway."

"If you know him that go talk to him," urged Alana.

"Would you ask him for me? He might have a girlfriend already," Responded Miranda shyly.

"No, I don't think he does," Alana said quickly.

"How do you know?"

"Um…I saw him standing alone with a bored expression on his face meaning…that he is looking for some company."

Miranda looked at Alana suspiciously. Alana had the feeling she knew this was risky talk, but it was worth a try. She did feel awful about pushing Miranda a bit, but it was for Miranda's own good. Miranda floated to a nearby window and saw that Moe was indeed standing along looking like he needed some company, exactly as Alana had said. Alana felt relieved and Jackie could see that.

"Well, I will go inside, but you two have to come."

"Promise," said Jackie.

They almost had to heave Miranda through the doors because at first she refused to go in. They made their way to where Moe was standing.

"Hello," he said, in a deep gentle voice. He looked very bored watching the gods and goddesses float by in many different directions or just dance to the pop music playing in the background. Alana recognized it as a song by *The Planettes*. She was disappointed that it wasn't Solarverse but the song had a striking beat. Jackie noticed that Miranda stood about a yard away from her but she gave off the impression that Moe was radioactive.

"So why aren't you dancing? Aren't you having a good time?" Jackie asked Moe, hoping to break the ice.

"That's what Lexana Venus said earlier," Moe pointed at a goddess who was dancing with a blond god in blue robes. She wore rosy colored robes with long wavy light brown hair that almost reached to the floor. Her jewel pattern was made up of pink sapphires with a hot pink heart in the center of the pattern. On Lexana's head was a gold crown meaning that she must be the princess. She looked at them, waved, then floated over to where they were, and said, "Would you like to join us now?"

"No thanks," Moe said. "We're fine."

"Alright." Lexana floated back to the blond god she was originally dancing with.

"So why are you standing here?" Alana asked Miranda. She looked around at everyone in the room dancing and enjoying themselves. There was more than enough space for fifty or more people. The music playing (this time it was Solarverse), could get a corpse dancing. There were even snacks on silver trays on which Jackie and Miranda started munching. She couldn't see any problem.

"Well things like this happen a lot and I just need some time to myself," Miranda said. "Everyone gets up and is so hyper, but these dances happen too often and they get boring."

"Well it might be easier when someone is here to talk to you," said Jackie who had been trying to get Miranda to come out of her shell. Now it looked as if Miranda had no choice. Jackie had been trying to get her to this point so hard the hat she was wearing had almost fallen off her head. Moe seemed to brighten up a little bit when he heard Miranda. Jackie threw Alana a smirk.

"Let's leave them alone," whispered Alana. They left the room inconspicuously as Moe and Miranda began chatting. They left feeling their work there was complete. Alana thought she saw Miranda's hair turn a cherry scarlet.

It would be fun to be friends with a goddess thought Alana as she and Jackie left the clouds and floated back to earth. Little did the girls know that having a goddess to protect them would be something that they would soon need.

 **Daze on the Set**

Dear Alana,

I get acne all the time and my face breaks out faster than when I can snap my fingers. No matter how many products I use, the pimples never go away. I don't want to live through middle school with the label 'Speed bump.'
-Crater face

Dear Anonymous, (I don't want to start with labels)

If there are no products that work for you, then ask your parents if you can go see a doctor. Special doctors can cure the worst acne cases. It sounds like you've tried everything but skin problems vary from person to person. Everyone (even movie stars) get pimples, but they just touch them up with makeup in the worst cases so you can't see the problem. Whatever happens know that you are more than just your looks. -Alana ☺

"Wake up Jackie!" Alana woke up with a start when she heard her dad call her name.

Alana realized that she and Jackie must have dozed off while the two girls were daydreaming. Jackie yawned and stood up with strands of hair in her face.

As the two girls walked back to Alana's house, they saw Alana's father with a briefcase in his hand. He was in some sort of rush. Alana was the only child of Bob and Kathleen Shannonson, as well as their pride and joy. Ever since she was a little girl Alana and her dad had a very special, sharing and playful relationship. Her parents were once concert musicians, but now her father was a business manager of a talent agency who helped a number of "special clients."

"I'm glad I found you," Alana's father said to them. "Your mom isn't home so I'll have to take you with me and besides you might really like what you see."

"In that case I'll bring my camera," said Alana. She turned to Jackie and whispered, "Every time he says you will like what you see I know it's something really cool. He never tells me right away, but always keeps me guessing," Alana added as the three squeezed themselves into her father's dark blue Porsche.

"Where are we going, Mr. Shannonson?" Jackie asked with innocent curiosity.

"I said you'll see, but actually I should say, you'll hear." Mr. Shannonson adjusted his reading glasses and patted his combed black hair.

The car arrived at a large white concrete building with a number of other cars already at the parking lot. When they walked into the building, the first thing that caught Alana's eye was a number of cameras, most of them with a camera crew nearby. A sign overhead said Cow Daze Stage. This caused Jackie to squeal with delight. The band was playing their theme song.

> *When there are outlaws on the loose*
> *There's one crew for the job*
> *You know they'll never stop*
>
> *Y'all know they've got the stuff*
> *For them varmints play rough*
> *Every time they end up in cuffs*
>
> *It's time to call the sheriff*
> *He'll lock 'em up tight*
> *If they escape again*
> *Our crew puts up a whoopin' good fight*
>
> *On the Cow Daze*
> *Say Howdy*
> *On the Cow Daze*
> *Gettin' through the maze*
>
> *YEE HAW*

"Hey look there's the director," Jackie pointed out a tall man sitting in a large chair labeled DIRECTOR CHARLES. Steven Charles was the director for the show. He wore a white shirt with black pants. In his hand were a script and a bottle of water. He was talking to the cast.

"Misty, I have said it before...you have to lasso the bull around the neck and you don't REALLY hit him," he said to one of the cast members.

"I have to make it look convincing, replied Misty Night, the young star of the show. *(Cow Daze* was a popular show about a young girl's life on a dairy farm in Texas.) "His curly hair makes it hard to know when to lift my hand. I have been practicing a lot with this lasso."

"This is the last scene in the episode this week so I know that we are all under a little stress. Everyone take 10. That's minutes, please." He looked at Misty who just shrugged.

He looked at Alana who had been taking pictures of the cast and said, "Sorry miss, pictures have to wait until after the shoot." Alana put her camera in its case and thought, *at least I got some great shots.* Her dad took her and Jackie over to meet Steven Charles, who looked really frazzled. Steven Charles had been the director of the show for five years. The show was wildly successful, but very difficult to direct. (You try getting a cow to act.)

Steven turned to Mr. Shannonson. "Showbiz is difficult work sometimes especially when there are conflicts among the cast members," he said. "I can't fire anybody because all the actors have big contracts and it would cost us over a million dollars to replace them. I wish that the cast conflicts could be resolved by a simple fix or action. So Bob do you have the papers?"

Mr. Shannonson reached for his briefcase, turned to Steven Charles and said, "Before we go over these, I would like to introduce you to my daughter Alana and her friend Jackie. Alana runs a very popular advice column in her school's newspaper."

"That's nice to hear," Steve said to Alana. "Maybe you have some advice you can give me," he said half jokingly.

"What exactly do you mean by conflicts in the cast?" replied Alana.

"Catfights, drama, focus issues.... the usual."

"Maybe I *can* help. I come across the same problems in my school. If I can come up with a solution for you, the shooting will go a lot easier."

Steven Charles thought for a minute and said, "All right, I guess it can't hurt. Misty is your own age. The dressing rooms are down the hall to the left. If you can find a solution, I'll let you take all the pictures you want. I don't usually do this but let's give it a try. But please, no photos in the dressing room unless permission is given by the actors. Oh, and one more thing. Please do not yell at anyone, we don't want any further disturbances. I've had enough of that already."

"Wow. Thanks a whole lot. I'll see what I can do," Alana replied, grinning excitedly.

"Oh my god, are we really going to see Misty Night's dressing room?" squealed Jackie.

"Yes, we are but we have to be calm and quiet just as Mr. Charles said."

They found their way to Misty Night's dressing room and knocked on the door. A melancholy voice said, "come in."

Alana and Jackie walked in to find a massive room painted pink with a floor length mirror in front of a large closet which held the many costumes and outfits that Misty used on the set. In the corner by the door there was a makeup desk and another huge mirror surrounded by lights under a sparkly pink clock. Some music was playing faintly in the background. On the walls were pictures of Misty's family, friends, the cast, and her pets. Misty, still in her costume, was lying down on a lavender couch twiddling her braids.

Alana didn't know quite what to say, but she had promised Mr. Charles that she would help. "Is there something wrong or something we can do to cheer you up?" Alana said to Misty. At this point, Alana had to be the one to talk because Jackie looked speechless like she didn't even believe she was even on Earth.

Misty looked at the two girls, "And who are you and how did you get into my dressing room? she asked.

"I am Bob Shannonson's daughter, Alana, and this is my friend Jackie. We're here with my dad and just thought we could meet you to talk. Mr. Charles said it was okay. You probably don't see too many kids your own age around the set."

"You're right, I don't," replied Misty. "I guess it would be nice to talk with someone who is not in show business for a change. It's just that the stress of taping the show on a very tight schedule every week causes everyone to pick on each other if things don't go according to schedule. If you only knew how many fights go on between us. Today it was just too much to handle," sighed Misty.

Alana replied, "Everyone has days like that in our school as well. We have to deal with this one mean girl who can't be avoided because she is everywhere. Kids get very upset with all the tension, and then they get moody as well. I would guess that stage directors are supposed to be strict, so don't feel as if you're being picked on." Misty sat up and smiled a little bit.

"Well everyone on the set gets along fairly well usually. Most of the time, we only fight on the set when we are filming under pressure. Mr. Charles is a very fair director and everyone here is treated equally."

"So if you know that, then what is bothering you?" asked Alana.

"It feels like I don't have enough time for things I'd like to do at home. When I try to schedule some time with my friends, there always seems to be something that has to be done for the show. That's why I can't seem to use the lasso properly. There just isn't enough time to practice everything and still be just a regular teen. I do want the show to keep its high ratings, but I also want to see my family and friends more. My family can't come to the set because they're working. My friends can't come because they have after-school activities or they are with *their* families."

Jackie meanwhile, who was muttering over and over again, "Wow, this is amazing, this is amazing," finally seem to come to her senses. She stopped staring around the room but it appeared that the fact that she was actually in her favorite celebrity's dressing room still seemed to block her ability to speak.

Alana realized she couldn't rely on Jackie to say anything. "Why don't you schedule time in advance when you are all free and just stick to it. That way you can still see your friends and family but not feel so stressed out," suggested Alana.

"That just might work," Misty replied. "I could think about making sure I had some time available for my family and friends."

Jackie asked, "Are you feeling better now?"

"Yes," replied Misty, "I am."

Alana looked at the clock. The break was almost over but the time on the clock didn't worry her. If this needed more time she would willingly take an extra minute. Hopefully this wouldn't take too long. Misty also glanced at the clock.

"We should go back to the set because the break is almost over."

"Maybe this episode will finish as planned," suggested Jackie.

"That would be great," Misty sighed hopefully.

As they wandered in back to the stage, Misty and everyone else got into place as the cameramen were setting up. Steven Charles began giving directions to everyone on and off the set.

"Is everyone ready?" He finally said. There were nods from the group.

"Start the camera in 5...4...3...2...1, start." The scene began and Misty lassoed the bull around the neck on the very first try. He put up a struggle as the others cornered him so he couldn't get away. The sheriff rode up to on a horse and locked the bull up in the clink. He was plotting his revenge (like in every episode) and laughed evilly. The show was finished at last, and in record time.

"And, that's a rap!" Steven Charles finished with a movement of his hand. "This will air in a few weeks so I hope you like the finished version."

As the cast headed for their dressing rooms Steven Charles said to Alana and Jackie, "Thanks girls, whatever you two did, you made the last scene go much easier. It only took 20 minutes."

"We're very happy to have helped," replied Alana.

"It wasn't any trouble," added Jackie.

Mr. Shannonson emerged from a nearby office. "I have delivered all of the papers for Mr. Charles, so we are free to leave now," he said to the girls.

He led Alana and Jackie off the stage. Jackie gave Alana another smirk. Alana didn't notice because she was reviewing all the pictures she had taken. All three got into Mr. Shannonson's car and drove off.

Alana did not notice, but her favorite necklace was no longer around her neck.

The Naughty New Neighbor

Dear Alana,

I get star struck even when I just look at pictures of movie stars. It seems like they get the glamorous life and I'm just bland. I would like to be an actress, but my brother makes fun of the idea. I have to put up with his comments since we are in the same school. I want to have a life as amazing as a movie star's, but it seems like that dream has exploded. -Stars in my eyes

Dear Stars,

Millions of fans get star struck and movie stars get "fan struck." Don't let your brother get in the way of achieving your dream. You have to be good at something so stick with your dream. Before you know it you will be number one. Remember don't act too obsessed with the idea because celebrities are just people too. -Alana ☺

Alana asked her father to drop them off at Jackie's house for the next few hours. They liked to explore the woods across from her house and have picnics in the meadow behind the path. Jackie's mom always let them hike alone because the girls were old enough. Sometimes the girls were asked to bring along Jackie's 6-year-old neighbor, Melissa, an energetic girl who wore her short black hair in barrettes and always managed to keep her hair out of her small round face. Today she wanted to come along so Alana and Jackie agreed. They were fond of Melissa's company but sometimes she was a handful. While they were walking to Melissa's house, Alana noticed a lot of boxes outside a house that was recently for sale.

"I didn't know you have new neighbors Jackie," Alana said.

"Yes, they have two girls. One is six and the other is seventeen. Their last name is Victor, and they officially moved in yesterday."

"Have you met them?"

"Yes, I met everyone except for the older girl, at a party Melissa's family had for them before they moved in. I think they are very nice."

Alana and Jackie approached Melissa's house and waited for her to come outside. When Melissa came out she was looking very cross. Her arms were folded on her chest, she had a frown on her brown face, and she walked with a stomp.

"I'm very mad today," Melissa exclaimed.

"Why, what happened?" Jackie asked.

"That new girl, Wendy is mean."

"What did she do to you?" asked Alana.

"She bossed me around, played with my Barbie doll, and bragged 'cause she thinks her sister is some big famous person."

"So you're saying she is bossy, rude and a liar?"

"She says her sis is in some stupid, famous music group called, The Planets."

"I think you mean, *The Planettes*. She's right about them being popular but that doesn't mean she can boss you around," Jackie replied gently. Jackie and Alana thought it was cute how the new girl Wendy could make up a story about the most popular band in the world right now.

"When I said you can't boss me, she said it was a free country and she can do what she wants to," replied Melissa angrily.

"Why don't we go over to her house and clear this up," Alana suggested.

"Fine but *I'm* not talking to her."

The three girls walked back to the house with the SOLD sign on the front lawn and knocked on the wooden door. A tall girl with long brown hair and green eyes opened the door. She wore a shiny gold tee shirt with a denim skirt, and had a golden necklace with the letters VV on it. Alana easily recognized her from the CD covers she owned even if she didn't have on her futuristic costume.

"Hi, is there anything I can do?" She spoke with a voice that sounded just like her soprano singing voice.

Alana and Jackie were shocked. There standing in the doorway was Vanessa Victor (a.k.a. Vanessa Venus), lead singer of *The Planettes*. Wendy was not lying at all. Her sister was indeed a big pop star.

"Uh...Hi, I'm...Shana Alananson,...no, ...I mean, Alana Shannonson, and these are my friends uh, um...(Alana couldn't remember their names) Jackie Donner and Melissa Huberton," said Jackie finishing Alana's sentence. "Is Wendy home?"

"Sure she is. I'll go get her." Vanessa went into the house.

"Oh my gosh! That's really Vanessa Victor!" exclaimed Alana.

"Yes and she seems very nice," Jackie said. "No need to get all ga-ga."

"Who?" asked Melissa.

Jackie was right thought Alana. No need to go star crazy. Melissa didn't even know who she was. Vanessa returned dragging a very steamed 6-year-old girl. She and Melissa stared angrily at each other tapping their feet.

"I heard they didn't get along very well at the party," Vanessa said.

"No, they didn't," said Jackie. To Melissa she whispered, *"Say you're sorry."*

"I'm sorry I took away the doll," Melissa offered.

"I'm sorry about pulling the head off, but I put it back together," said Wendy. She handed Melissa a very well-dressed Barbie doll in a blue dress with matching shoes. Melissa brightened up as she hugged the doll tightly.

I don't think I want to know what really happened, thought Alana. *At least they didn't have a fist fight.*

"My fight with Melissa was not *that* bad," Wendy said. "If you really want to see a fight, then you should go to the music place where Vanessa works. She said there are problems and yelling there," Wendy exclaimed proudly.

"You know," said Vanessa, "you girls did such a great job of solving the fight between Melissa and Wendy, perhaps you two can fix the problems on the set for the next Solarverse Music Video Show. I was about to leave to head over there. Perhaps you can come with me. Maybe the music video series for Solarverse will finally finish on a up note.

"Sure, we'd love to go," replied Alana, now all excited.

"Okay, but first I'll have to call the producer and ask him."

"We'll have to call your mom too," Alana said to Jackie.

"Overall I don't think that there would be any trouble getting you two on the set, but you will need passes," Vanessa replied. She took out some laminated passes from her pocket. She put one over her own neck and gave the other two to Alana and Jackie who exchanged glances as they put the passes over their necks.

"Can you call your parents now so we can leave?" Vanessa asked Jackie. After Jackie got permission from her mom, they hopped into Vanessa's convertible and were off to the studio." This time, however, the girls would be in for their biggest advice challenge

When Worlds Collide

Dear Alana,

I don't get the best grades because I'm so busy with after-school activities. For me there aren't enough hours in the day. My single mom works all day so I can't get extra help before school. Other kids are beginning to think I'm an idiot when I'm not. -No Time to Study

Dear No Time,

I'm a perfectionist about my grades, so I know what it's like when a project's grade isn't what you believe you should get. Why don't you ask for help from your mom about the things you don't understand when you are home together at night? She'll be more than willing to help out so she can spend more time with you. If you think you are too busy with after school activities give up a few. You should ride the bus and relax more often and really consider drop the activities that are slowing you down. -Alana ☺

Today has been just one adventure after another, thought Alana as she remembered what she and Jackie had just gone through. Jackie kept grinning all through the ride in the car. Alana thought it was because of the many cool experiences they've had in one day. Now they were off to their favorite band's music studio for the taping of a show. Nothing could possibly ruin today.

Vanessa left Jane and Jackie off by the entrance as she went to park the car in the Star's lot. Alana's smile faltered when they got to the studio door. There, just outside was Jane Luklit strutting around the parking lot with two brightly colored passes in her hands similar to those Alana, and Jackie were wearing around their necks. Jane was next to Sean Pedene. Jane and Sean sauntered over to where Alana and Jackie stood.

"What are *you* doing *here*?" Jane asked Alana with utter disdain in her voice. Jane looked over to Sean, who was standing next to her and said sarcastically, "Don't the security guards know to keep away snoops and pests?"

"Don't worry Jane, you'll be gone in no time," Alana huffed. She was tempted to take a peek to the left of her to see how Sean reacted, but she resisted.

"At least I am smart enough to bring someone decent with me who, like, knows how to dress." Jane pointed her manicured finger at Jackie's sky blue bandana and wrapped the other arm around Sean's as she rolled her eyes skyward.

"Why do you always have to trash-talk and put someone down?" Alana retorted, hoping she could make Jane realize what she was doing.

"If you are so perfect, why do you have to insult a *poor* girl like me, who just wants to be happy about winning these backstage passes and bring a date to a big show?" Jane replied in a sugar sweet voice as she briskly waved her tickets in Alana's face.

Alana couldn't care less about the tickets. It wasn't the fact that Jane had tickets, it was the fact that Jane, the drama queen, was always nearby, no matter where Alana went. She seemed unavoidable and she chose to deliberately ignore the fact that Alana and Jackie were also sporting the same passes.

"Well I'd love nothing more than to continue chatting, but Sean and I have to go inside before *The Planettes* start without us and what a tragic loss that would be...for them!" Jane said as she sashayed inside.

"See ya, Alana," Sean said meekly as he followed Jane. The heavy perfume Jane wore left a trail. Alana couldn't help but cough. She noticed Jackie and Sean did the same and wasn't the least bit surprised.

"If I were a guard for two minutes...," she thought. *"But I can't let that trash-talking poser ruin my day."*

Jackie was mad too. Her eyes flashed fiercely as if she thought to herself, *I bet I'll see her in the same bandana on Tuesday or Monday. What a phony! She doesn't even like* pop music but knows The Planettes *are one of Sean's favorite bands. The devil in cosmetics strikes again.*" she said to herself.

As Alana and Jackie were cooking up even more thoughts, Vanessa finally returned a minute later wearing a scarf to hide herself. She did this to avoid being mobbed by the fans going to the concert.

"We have to go inside now. You will have to go in from this door. I have to get in my costume with Missy and Natasha." Vanessa ushered Alana and Jackie inside through a backstage entrance. "Just follow the signs along the hallways. When you get to the stage set, read the number on the back of the card." The two girls followed the directions well. Alana looked at the back of the pass and the numbers said, **Row A, Seat 1**.

Jackie looked at hers. She was in row A and seat 2. Looking around, they realized that those were the best seats. They got to their seats. They heard yelling and complaining from the door a few rows back.

"What do you mean no flash photography? I demand an explanation! If you won't let me take the pictures I deserve, I'll sue!" said some woman that looked important.

"You'd better turn the flash off your camera," whispered Jackie. "You know what will happen if a guard catches you. He'll take your camera and when Jane sees that...you'll get five days of dissing."

"You're right, I'd rather be sent to prison than have that kind of abuse," muttered Alana. She adjusted her digital camera setting. It was almost silent in the room. Besides her, Jackie, Jane, and Sean there were about five others who got to see the music videos from the front section. Fortunately Alana and Jackie's passes also gave them the right to go backstage during or after the show. Thirty minutes crawled by but there was still no sign of *The Planettes* or the stage crew. She could hear Jane whispering to Sean.

"I took valuable time off my busy schedule and this is what happens."

"Relax, they always take extra time to change and tune their instruments.

"They better get here soon," grumbled Jane.

Alana whispered to Jackie, "They don't usually take this long."

"Let's go backstage and find out what's up." Alana and Jackie got up from their seats and passed by the guard. When they got backstage, they sensed a lot of tension in the air between everyone. There were piles of strings, wires, electric devices, and boxes strewn about.

The Planettes were all dressed up in their silver costumes with necklaces, bracelets and their own personal colors. There were shiny, golden tints for Vanessa, matching light blue shades for Natasha, and stunning red streaks for Missy. They looked a lot like the photo on their CD cover except the costume designs and cuts were different. They seemed all prepared for the show but nothing seemed to be happening.

"The stage crew isn't ready," Natasha said.

"They can't agree on what special effects to use," added Vanessa.

"So we don't have our cue to come out and start," finished Missy.

"Where is the crew?" suggested Alana. "Maybe we can help."

"That's probably not the best idea," cautioned Natasha.

"Why not?" asked Jackie.

"They get very irritated when they think someone is trying to tell them how to do their job."

"We don't want to tell them off or anything. We just want to give them a few suggestions."

"They are up in the control room trying to work out the lighting, sound system and can't seem to decide on what effects they need," replied Missy. "Steven Charles isn't pleased."

"Wait did you say, Steven Charles?" Alana asked.

"Yes, he works with us when we make music videos, sing in movies, or make guest appearances on his show Cow Daze."

"Why do they use the actual band and not just use a soundtrack for the songs from the Cow Daze show?"

Natasha replied, "Mr. Charles says having the band there creates much more energy and is better for the show. Besides, the song sounds better when the band actually sings, it's more natural. It also sometimes gives the show and the production company more publicity. Do you know Steven Charles?"

"Well I know Mr. Charles a little bit because my dad works for him, so he might be open to some ideas. How I know him is kind of a long story. Where is he right now?"

"He's up in the control room two flights up the stairs, down the first hallway, and the third door on the right," replied Vanessa.

"All right thanks."

"We are really getting a lot of exercise today aren't we?" Jackie sighed, breathlessly.

"At last...we reached the control room," muttered Alana. The girls could clearly hear the yelling going on about the direction and effects from where they were standing outside the door.

"You have to do the shooting star effect first because it will be like a wish come true when the band starts singing." argued Joey Martin, the lighting director.

"The shooting star will work better after they start singing because then the audience will want to see more. The universe effect is better to start with because the song is called Solarverse, and we need a large space because the song is about a large world or at least it features one," replied Nat Donough, the control room director.

"Solarverse is about a large world filled with good luck that can be found if we believe in ourselves. We need something big, bright and lucky that swirls around the band but doesn't take away the girls' image," said Steven Charles, not wishing to over rule his two temperamental associates.

"Oh brother...this sounds so familiar," Alana thought.

"That's why I say a shooting star or a crowd of them. I've been in this business for ten years and this is the band's second music video. Mr. Charles, I know what will look good," said Joey.

"I know Joey, but you and Nat have to decide on something or at least compromise. You both have good ideas but I can't decide for you."

Alana and Jackie realized that this fighting had to end. Everyone, including Jane were down below in their seats. If she started complaining about the delay going on Alana and Jackie would never hear the end of it. So they knocked on the door. Inside they could see that the room was less cluttered than backstage but people still needed to watch where they stepped.

"I couldn't help overhearing the problems up here," Alana told three surprised men. She recognized Steven Charles from the Cow Daze set. One of the other two men, Joey was tall, had black hair and was wearing a gray shirt with STAFF written on the front, and khakis. The other, Nat, was shorter had brown hair and wore a dark blue Yankees cap with a plain, blue shirt and jeans.

"Hey, Alana what brings you here?" asked Steven Charles. To the other men he muttered, "This is Bob Shannonson's daughter, Alana and her friend, Jackie."

"I heard there were problems up here. I could tell by the delay."

"Well we are working out the effects for *The Planettes* music video and there are so many good things to choose from but we can use a limited amount."

"Well may we help? We might be able to help you find what you're looking for," added Jackie.

"Well, replied Steven Charles, I still owe you for helping out on the Cow Daze set, but this is a lot of work. We plan to air this video tonight at 9:00 P.M. on channel 100 if we can finish in time."

"We'll handle it. It's a lot like working on the school newspaper," offered Alana.

"Well we can't decide whether we should use the universe or a swirl of shooting stars."

"From the looks of the video, I think *The Planette*s should arrive with the shooting stars and then stand in the Universe or at least the Solar System and maybe have some shooting stars and comets in the background passing by so it adds to the part of Solarverse being a lucky place. I think there should be different camera angles of the different girls and at the end I think that there should be an angel smiling and the stars blinking out. Did you follow all that?"

"Well some of that we have, but we like that new idea of the stars blinking out,"

Joey and Nat nodded in agreement. "We can set it that way, as it makes sense." The two men offered. "We might use some of those ideas for the final thing. This will appear on the internet and TV soon."

"Do you want us to tell Vanessa, Natasha, and Missy they can now sing their song?" asked Jackie.

"Go ahead! And, sorry about the delay. By the way, thanks for the help, I don't know how to repay you," Mr. Charles said, taking the girls picture when they were not looking.

"It's fine." said Alana.

Alana and Jackie made it back to the stage in no time and gave the girls the message. They then found their seats and settled in. Finally, they were going to hear their favorite band perform live.

When they were finished with Solarverse, *The Planettes* gave the audience a treat and sang a song, Starlets from their new album that was going to be released a month from that Saturday.

What do you see when you look at us
Singers and dancers and maybe stars
There is more that what you see
There is more that there will be

If you think that stars are easily bright
And you try with all your might
There are lots you have to do
Believe it we're not stars yet
We'd be what you'd call Starlets

Stars in the sky, looking so high
That's where I want to be
At the top and the peak of the point
Sun giving light Moon shining bright
I want to shine and still be me

If you think that stars are easily bright
And you try with all your might
There are lots you have to do
Believe it we're not stars yet
We'd be what you'd call Starlets

The colors all around
From the sun to the ground
Gives off a feeling that can't be described
Maybe a calm passion
Or a placid vibe
Only a fraction of the feelings of the sky

If you think that stars are easily bright
And you try with all your might
There are lots you have to do
Believe it we're not stars yet
We'd be what you'd call Starlets

The audience cheered as loud as they could and the
room echoed like it was a concert hall. The singers took
their bows. Missy and Natasha threw wristbands with their
band's logo of the Solar System that looked like this:

Everybody seemed happy, but the girls would soon find out what thanks really meant.

"Could this get any better?" asked Jackie as a wristband thrown from the stage almost knocked off her bandana.

"Yes, I could think of a way," said Alana, looking back a few rows.

Jane was still cross. Her foot was tapping impatiently and her arms were folded on her chest. She reminded Alana of how Melissa had looked. Obviously, Jane hated the concert, but it was her own fault so she couldn't blame anyone. She muttered to herself as most of the crowd filed out while everyone else got signed posters of the band. Alana and Jackie waited for Vanessa in the parking lot. When she finally arrived she drove Alana and Jackie back to Jackie's house. They thanked her for everything as they recalled every adventure that happened that day.

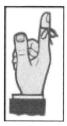

Recollection

Dear Alana,

    People criticize me all of the time. I get gossiped about but it's never true! I know that middle school is tough but this is way out of line. Almost every girl is nasty to me and sometimes the guys are perverted and nasty (well at least the ones I know). I can't help the way I grow or act sometimes.
-Frazzled

Dear Frazzled,

    Everyone is entitled to his or her own opinion. Just don't let it get to you. Don't make the judgement that "all girls" are this or that "all guys" are that, just because a few are bad. What you can do is just hang out with your real friends and zone out the lies outside your circle of friends.. -Alana ☺

Alana and Jackie sat on the couch in her basement. Like every room in Jackie's house it was big with at least one place on which to relax. Jackie's parents believed in giving children a lot of room to express themselves. Her mother was a teacher and her father was a scientist at EARTH'N Tech Inc., which created technology for improving the human mind.

They recounted everything that had happened that day.

"Boy today wasn't exactly what I expected," sighed Alana. "First, on the *Treasure Hunter,* then up in the sky into one of my stories, then onto the set of Cow Daze, and THEN just when we go to have a picnic we end up seeing...rather making, the video for Solarverse."

"I consider this a great long weekend," Jackie replied. "And I saw that you got some great pictures. May I see?"

They looked at the many pictures Alana had taken of the Cow Daze stars, Jackie, Melissa, *The Planettes* and even Sean Pedene. Alana even took a video of Jane in the parking lot and on the set, but after she and Jackie had a good laugh, she deleted it.

"You'd make a great photographer for the *Walk Street Journal* but you also make a good advice columnist as well."

"Well, maybe, but I still can't always think of good advice to give to everyone all of the time. I usually do well, but not always."

"Perhaps you need a rest," suggested Jackie who looked slightly disappointed. "Your parents are letting us have a sleepover tonight or else they wouldn't have dropped off a pair of pajamas at my front door that clearly aren't mine."

"Yes, double dose of Donner!" cheered Alana.

"Get the party started. Let's go upstairs. You might really like what you see."

"Jackie, I know what your room looks like: Aqua blue walls, plush carpeting, two wide wooden beds, a sky blue closet with a mirror, and a huge bandanna/hat collection on an oversized coat hanger with your CDs on a shelf next to it."

"Of course that's what it looked like last time, but there are updates."

As they entered Jackie's room Alana's jaws dropped open. Jackie had added a large silver disco ball that hung from the center of her ceiling. The poster of *The Planettes* was put up next to the mirror on Jackie's closet and an enlarged picture of Alana and Jackie was proudly placed on the door.

"Oh my god, this is so cool." Alana sighed.

"What do you want to do?" "Would you like to use the disco ball and dance?"

"Yes, why don't we listen to Himcules for a change and then listen to Helligant." Himcules was a muscular, pop rock singer who dressed like Hercules, only Americanized by wearing sandals that didn't tie and wristbands instead of metal bands. Like the famous Greek god he wore a complete armored suit. He was popular among girls because of his attire and muscles. Alana and Jackie were not as attracted to Himcules as some people in their school, namely Jane, however they did enjoy his rock music. Helligant, on the other hand, was a popular teen punk band wannabe featuring the lead singer Charlene Scarlette, an auburn-haired teen with a keen voice and sharp lyrics. The guitar players were Jesse Spider and Karla Weller, who were both blonde and rocked out on their electric guitars. Their drummer was Mark Barrs, who was brown-haired, fast-fingered, and a real source of energy. The song Jackie played was called Earthquake by Himcules.

Hear the rumble of the rocks
See the shake of the Earth
The Storm is approaching
So find a place to hide

Thunder rumbling fiercely
Lightening blinding
You don't want to be near
This stormy guy

Where to hit
Where to strike next
Where is the perfect place for the storm to hit?
Wherever the traitor lies

Why doesn't he show himself?
Where are you hiding?
Crooks can't hide forever
Sooner or later without a doubt
You will have to come out

I will find out where you have hidden
And the truth will be told
You are the guilty one
Any not who you framed
He has a heart of gold

Where to hit
Where to strike next
Where is the perfect place for the storm to hit?

Wherever the traitor lies

Why doesn't he show himself?
Where are you hiding?
Crooks can't hide forever
Sooner or later without a doubt
You will have to come out

"Now let's to listen to Helligant's smash hit, Gravitation Zero," announced Alana, trying to sound like a radio disc jockey.

I'm no longer on planet earth
Where I'm chained to the ground
I am now free to go to the moon
A zero gravity place I think I've found

Hey!
Ho!
On gravitation zero,
Hey, Ho!
You should all know.
Free zone,
On gravitation zero.

No longer locked on heavy gravity
With no space to move around
Free on my own space, my own place
A zero gravity place I know I've found

Hey!
Ho!
On gravitation zero
Hey, Ho!
You should all know.
Free zone!
On gravitation zero!

I finally know where to spend my life
No more crowds and full of time
A planet unspoiled and totally mine
Open space on my own place
No more evil in this maze
As here I'll spend many days

Hey!
Ho!
On gravitation zero
Hey, Ho
You should all know
Free zone!
On gravitation zero!

I located where I belong
I feel on top just like King Kong
I lost a little and gained a lot
I've gotten off at my spot
Located right on the dot

Hey!
Ho!
On gravitation zero,
Hey, Ho!
You should all know.
Free zone,
On gravitation zero!

Hey!
Ho!
On gravitation zero,
Hey, Ho!
You should all know.
Free zone,
On gravitation zero.

Hey Ho! Hey Ho! Hey Ho!

"Let's listen to more," encouraged Alana. "Gravitation Zero is still buzzing in my head."

For the next hour Alana and Jackie listened to more of their favorite bands, including *The Planettes*. They even sang along to their favorite songs and danced. Jackie's disco ball made the effects more interesting. They reminded her of stars in the solar system.

"Jackie, what time did Mr. Charles say they wanted to air the video?"

"He said about nine o'clock...what time is it?"

"It's 8:55 and we better hurry to your living room."

The girls hurried to Jackie's living room where they pressed the remote button and saw the rest of a TV rerun before Solarverse came on. The video started with long-tailed, glimmering, shooting stars and comets as the entrance. *The Planettes* came on playing the introduction of the song with an occasional comet in the background. The story of the music video was a sad little girl (played by Wendy Victor) who was having a hard time at school making friends. She looked out the window and saw some bright stars winking at her. *The Planettes* were playing and singing in the sky. Wendy closed her eyes and made a wish. She turned and there was another girl (to Alana and Jackie's surprise the second girl was Melissa Huberton). There were a few camera angles of the Melissa, Wendy and then back to *The Planettes*. At the end, the two girls came together and smiled. Then the picture changed from them to a picture of Alana and Jackie posed in the same way to a photo of some adults, who were probably relatives of the small girls. There was one more shot of *The Planettes* and they faded away so all that remained was the black night sky with stars blinking back and a shooting star streaked across the sky.

"Wow, we're in the video! When they said they were going to repay us, they didn't have to do something that big!" Jackie said excitedly.

"We need to thank Mr. Charles tomorrow and pay a visit to Vanessa," Alana added.

"I wonder why we didn't see Melissa or Wendy on the set."

"Probably because they covered that part in the beginning of the video shoot and we got to the set when they were finishing."

"Cow Daze comes on soon would you like to watch it as well?"

"No, it's a rerun. The last new episode is the season finale and that airs next week. I'd prefer to go back to your room and relax and maybe pay some attention to your lazy, lonely cat, James."

"OK, he's probably in my room somewhere and it's not very often that he gets visitors."

"You're sounding like a worker at a nursing home."

Alana and Jackie raced upstairs to Jackie's room to find a very large black cat snoozing on the rug near Jackie's bed. Next to it a young white kitten with a pink bow tied around her neck was napping and purring loudly.

"I didn't see them there when we first came into your room and since when did you get a white cat?"

"James must've come in while we were downstairs. I guess we're cat-sitting Colleen, my cousin Alyson's cat. We got James from their old cat before the poor old tabby died. It looks like we will have some company when we sleep tonight."

"They must've had a good day, listen to how loudly they purr."

The two napping cats were indeed purring loudly. Alana thought they looked like father and daughter and the daughter was following in her fathers footsteps.

"Looking at them makes me tired."

"Me too I could fall asleep now."

As the two girls got ready and climbed into the beds, Jackie slept in the bed on one side of the room and Alana the other. Jackie tried to tell Alana something important she had remembered, but she was fast asleep before she could say anything.

The Visit

Dear Alana,

I am on the cheerleading squad and I'm not as athletic as the other girls. We always have to do all kinds of flexible stunts but I can barely do a round-off. I don't want to be the person who kills us in the championship. Got any tips? - Athlete Wannabe

Dear Athlete,

You might need more practice on the stunts. Perhaps one of the other girls could help you out. If that doesn't work and you still want to be on the squad, ask to be an alternate or backup. If none of those work, the best thing to do is train until you can make the team. Hard work always pays off. --Alana ☺

Alana and Jackie slept late the next morning. It was well past 9:30 when Jackie got up and realized she had forgotten something important.

"Alana, get up! Hurry!" Jackie tossed her pillow at her head. Alana grudgingly got out of bed, moaning.

Jackie explained to Alana why they had to get up.

"I wake up early on a Sunday because we have to visit your neighbor?" Alana moaned after Jackie explained. "If they're still asleep we get to come back OK?"

Both girls got dressed, Alana in a shiny purple V-neck with jeans and Jackie in a light blue tee and denim shorts, topped by a light blue hat. They gulped down a breakfast of waffles with maple syrup and orange juice and rushed down the street. Alana and Jackie were completely out of breath when they got to Vanessa's house. When they knocked on the door, Vanessa answered yawning. She was wearing pink pajamas and her hair wasn't brushed.

"Hi, Sorry about how I look but Wendy woke me up too early."

Alana thought *join the club* but instead she said, "I know what that's like." She glared at Jackie who merely rolled her eyes.

"Please come in!" Vanessa led the girls into the kitchen. It was small yet inviting. The room gave the impression that the family was organized.

"We came to thank you for everything--from letting us see the music video to putting in a photo of us," Jackie said.

"That was Mr. Charles' idea. He said you helped so much that he had to thank you in some way. He and the other men let us see the video beforehand to see if there were any changes we needed to make but Missy and Natasha and I liked the video as much as they did."

"Thanks for letting us come to the set."

"Thanks for helping out."

"Is there any way to thank Mr. Charles?"

"My dad could help with that," yawned Alana. "He works at the set part of the time." Alana had been resting her head on the kitchen table the whole time and was pre-pared to doze off but Jackie kicked her foot under the table.

"Thanks for letting us come in Vanessa," Jackie said as she shook Alana's head to make sure she got the message. She reluctantly rose to leave and thanked Vanessa who merely waved good-bye.

As the two girls slowly walked home, Alana thought to herself what a great day it was yesterday. She reached down to touch her good luck necklace, but it was gone.

"Oh No!" she shrieked. "My jade stone necklace....it's gone!"

Todaze a Helligant Day

Dear Alana,
   I'm in the AV club and most of the others look down upon us "dorks" but I look and act nothing like the label. I'm just smart with technology. I hate labels and I'd like to know how to change mine. -NOT a soup can

Dear Soup,
   It doesn't matter what other people think of you. Some people just want to make themselves feel better by putting down others. If you don't care and just go about your business, then they will back off. Be confident with who you are and eventually those "others" will disappear and go find their next victim. --Alana ☺

Alana and Jackie scurried back to Jackie's house and after spending an hour frantically searching for the necklace. They finally asked Jackie's parents to drive them to Alana's house. Since parents always seemed ready to start the day early, (unlike Alana and Jackie) they eagerly agreed. Alana thanked them for having her over as they all rushed off back to Alana's house. They needed to either find the necklace or Mr. Shannonson because he was leaving for some business appointment. Alana and Jackie caught up with him just as he was getting into his Porsche.

"Hey Dad, wait. Where are you going?" puffed Alana, having now given up on finding the necklace at home.

   "Alana why are you up so early?" joked Mr. Shannonson. "Is it time to go to school already? I'm going to the Cow Daze set where they're filming new episodes for season four. It was because of you two I got a big new contract and a promotion."

"Congratulations Mr. Shannonson!" exclaimed Jackie.

"Nice joke Dad, now may we go to the set with you?" asked Alana. "I may have left my necklace there."

"All right, but please don't try to take over. I already have one boss and I don't think I can handle another. Now come on you two, get in!"

Alana rolled her eyes as Jackie laughed while Mr. Shannonson started the car. The girls climbed in as they made their way to the familiar white building. Through the mob of workers and cameramen the three found their way to Mr. Shannonson's new office. It was a large space with a window. There was a desktop computer and a color printer. A polished wooden cabinet was next to a large white board that included four different markers for making graphs. A set of drawers sat under the edge of the desk. Alana was so surprised at the size of the office, she was now completely awake. Out the window she saw a view of the forest and a small lake to the left of the parking lot.

"Wow! Is this really your new office because it looks great!" exclaimed Jackie.

"Unless you know another Bob Shannonson that works here, this is my office." He pointed to the door. There was a small black sign to the left that had his nameon it in white letters.

"We have 20 minutes until they need to shoot the beginning scene. So you two just make yourselves at home, but not too much. I need my own space, which I don't get in any of the rooms at home, if you know what I mean."

"What about the men's room?" teased Alana.

"Very funny you goofball, now why don't you and Jackie doodle on the whiteboard or something, because we have a little time before they call us down to the set?"

"Good idea!" Alana said, "Why don't we think of new episodes for the show. I see some lined paper next to the printer."

"Cool, maybe they'll use some of our ideas."

Alana and Jackie worked and brainstormed on the floor of the office and came up with some great ideas for some new episodes. One of Jackie's "brilliant" ideas (as Alana said) involved Helligant or Himcules singing in an episode since the studio already used *The Planettes.*

It hadn't been difficult to brainstorm everything because Alana and Jackie based their ideas on what happened to them in real life. Finally everyone had to go to the set for the taping of the show. Alana slipped her papers into her jeans pocket. Jackie did the same. They were hoping for a chance to recommend their ideas to Steven Charles if they got one.

"Places cast, crew, and cameramen," called out Mr. Charles through a megaphone. "Is every cowboy or cowgirl on set? Misty, Billy, Darcy. Derrick?" The actors nodded gingerly.

"Are the outlaws on the set? The Kid, Sandy, Cat L. Herder, Tornado?" The outlaws nodded fervently.

"OK, before starting this scene, let's go over the plot line one more time. The outlaws, working together, can control dry weather and can generate windstorms as well. Their aim is to steal the cattle from the good guys. Everybody get it? Let's begin. Start the camera in 5... 4... 3... 2...1...and Action!"

Tornado and Sandy aimed a sandstorm at Darcy and Billy, who were blown back so hard that they had no time to react. Misty tried to grab them with her lasso, but The Kid pushed her down and blew sand in her face so she wouldn't be able to help her friends before they landed hard. Derrick tried to take Cat L. Herder's gun away with her lasso, but before she could, the outlaws had stolen every last cow. Pleased with how they had succeeded, the outlaws fled on their horses in a rush of sand and wind with Cat leading away the herd of cattle.

"And cut!" called out Steven Charles. The cameras stopped rolling and about half a dozen workers started fixing up the set by adding or removing sand from a hidden bag that had caused the storm.

"Take a 10 minute break. We are way ahead of schedule this time." Alana and Jackie, who were fascinated with all the action on the set, decided that now was the right time to thank Mr. Charles for everything that he had done for them.

"Hi Mr. Charles, How's everything going?" asked Jackie.

"It's fine girls. How are you?"

"We are great and we want to say thanks for adding us to the Solarverse music video," replied Alana.

"I had to say thanks for all the help you've given me. You are just like your father, Alana, a hard worker, responsible and willing to make improvements."

She thought, *that's what Captain Arben said, but speaking of improvement...* Before she or Jackie forgot, Alana took out her papers with the episode ideas.

"We had some ideas for Cow Daze episodes." She and Jackie handed their papers to Steven Charles who didn't seem surprised as he read.

"Some of these are really good ideas and others we already are using. Speaking of Helligant, I am using them to sing in a future episode. We are thinking about using one of their band members to guest star in the end as the evil mastermind, although we might not actually make the commitment given the bands touring schedule."

"So are we going to hear them sing soon?" asked Jackie.

"Actually that's in the final scene but we weren't planning to do that one today unless we really need to. Just in case, we have Helligant rehearsing their song, Gravitation Zero, in the soundproof room in the back. We can't go back there unless someone calls us over the intercom to that area of the building."

"Wow!" It was the only thing Alana and Jackie could say as they imagined a mini concert with all the special effects going on in the rear of the studio. Both were really fascinated by the studio and everything that occurred around it. Alana could almost recollect Gravitation Zero word for word.

"Well, thanks again for everything," she remarked after a minute of daydreaming.

"Come anytime! Maybe when you two get old enough to work, you could be on our writing staff."

"First we have to turn 14," Alana joked as Jackie giggled. "Yeah and perhaps we should at least have taken English or be in high school? chuckled Jackie. Steven Charles looked at his digital watch and grabbed his megaphone from the director's chair and shouted, "Places everyone. We have to start shooting scene four. I repeat places for all people that are in scene four."

"Wouldn't it be easier to give the scenes creative titles as well as still use the scene numbers?" asked Alana after Steven Charles put down his megaphone.

"There you go again! This is only your second time here and you might have improved not only our ratings, but our work routines as well," Steven Charles added with a laugh. "Didn't your dad warn you not to take over?"

"He did, but I'm sure he was more afraid that I would get the promotion instead of him." Steven Charles chuckled and gave the cameramen directions and he called out again, "Are all the cowboys and cowgirls on the set? Misty, Darcy, Derrick, Billy?" The four nodded eagerly while Misty gave Alana and Jackie a smile.

"Roll camera in 5...4...3...2....1...WAIT STOP!" Everyone was confused and all of a sudden everyone in the room seemed to tense up. An assistant had walked up to Steven Charles and said that the actor playing the ranch owner couldn't make it to the set that day because he had the flu. Steven Charles cursed under his breath.

"Is Helligant ready to play Gravitation Zero?"

"They've been ready for a half hour."

"Bring them to the set but please don't mention anything over the intercom. Just go to the back room, the soundproof one." To the crowd Mr. Charles announced, "Take five."

Darcy, Derrick, and Billy went to their dressing rooms, but Misty strolled over to Alana and Jackie to say hello.

"I am glad to see you two again."

"We're glad to see you, too," replied Jackie.

"How's everything been going?" asked Alana.

"It's been going great and thanks to you I now see everyone at home more often," Misty answered.

"There haven't been any problems on the set?" Alana asked.

"Not until now. Fortunately for us, this is only minor so we won't get too far behind or maybe we can even stay ahead, as Mr. Charles mentioned."

"It's great that everything's going so well," responded Jackie.

"Would you like to meet everyone else?" Misty asked. "Darcy, Derrick and Billy are always pleased to meet loyal fans."

"That would be fantastic. We've always wanted to meet the entire cast or at least the cowboys and girls. Do you prefer to go by the group name, Rustler Hustlers?"

"Rustler Hustlers is an easier way to address us instead of saying all of our names. That's just what we use, and I wanted to know if you wanted to meet the others."

"Wow, we'd love to!" cried Alana who was so eager to personally get together with her favorite stars.

"We might not have enough time for question and answers but you will get to say hi." Misty turned and led the other group members, Darcy Adams, a good-natured brunette, Derrick Grannon, a lanky, laid-back looking guy with jet black hair and Billy Marliff, a tall, burly, guy with straw-colored hair.

"Guys, meet Alana Shannonson and Jackie Donner. They helped us a lot with the set and filming."

"Pleased to meet you at last, we've heard a lot about you from Mr. Charles and Misty," replied Darcy. Her high pitched voice reminded Alana of honey and sugar.

"Yeah I heard you have a pretty good sense of humor because your dad says that you both like to goof around," added Billy. "Your dad seems like someone who loves to tell jokes and sounds like he knows a lot about popular culture and entertainment."

"Thanks. Yeah dad's pretty cool. He knows a lot," replied Alana. "It's great to finally meet you all in person and not just on a glass screen. As far as I'm concerned seeing the action live is far more interesting than watching on TV. Before I forget, may I take a picture of the group...if none of you mind."

"I don't mind," responded Darcy.

"We don't mind," added Derrick who spoke in a fast but casual way. The Rustler Hustlers grouped together and Alana snapped a great photo.

"Thanks a lot."

"Anytime!"

Jackie looked from one actor to the next and said, "Acting in a show like Cow Daze must be extremely amazing, I mean you're working on such a successful show, are famous, make lots of money, and you have a good time all at the same time!"

"Well we do have a good time," Misty began, "but it's a lot of hard work memorizing lines and getting the action correct.

"A lot of times we're doing a scene over and over again," added Derrick.

"Sometimes we have to change the action slightly because we can't move the right way or memorize the dialogue in time," Darcy continued.

"But, in the end it's all worth it because we always put together a killer episode. At least that's what the crew tells us after every production," said Billy somewhat sarcastically.

"Everyone tells us how good we are so often that we actually start to believe it," finished Darcy, who seemed even at her young age to have a good understanding of the phoniness of the entertainment industry.

Alana thought, here's a girl that must be well grounded because she spoke about the business she was in with a sad laugh in her voice. Darcy had worked on a teen-famous TV show prior to Cow Daze, so she knew quite well what the actors and the people who make a living off of them were really like.

Alana suddenly felt like a reporter doing an interview. She always wanted a career in journalism and she decided if she didn't start her own advice column when she applied for a job she would become a reporter. She and Jackie were meeting celebrity actors and actresses so she could consider this her first official interview.

"It looks like Mr. Charles has the filming issue under control," observed Derrick.

The others looked to their right and saw Steven Charles talking to an assistant while some teens in black shirts with various logos and blue jeans were standing nearby tuning their instruments. Alana looked at Jackie and they were both thinking the same thing, *they look like they're ready for a concert.* Jackie's hat almost fell off she was so excited because there were so many important people crammed into the one stuffy room.

"We better get ready and alert the others because Mr. Charles looks ready to call our cues soon," warned Darcy.

"Good idea!" Misty turned to Alana and Jackie and said, "We have to get ready for the scene but it was nice to see you again."

"It was cool to see you too," responded Jackie.

"It was a pleasure meeting you," Alana called to Darcy, Billy and Derrick.

"Cool meeting you too!" replied Billy.

"Catch ya'll later," cried Derrick. Just as Darcy predicted, Steven Charles' voice came over his megaphone. "Are all the characters that are in the final scene in costume and on set?"

"Yes," replied everyone on the set from the Rustler Hustlers to the Outlaws as everyone seemed to be in a hurry to finish soon.

"Start the cameras in five, four, three, two, and one, ACTION!"

"Helligant performed their song enthusiastically and to Alana, the song sounded much different in person than on the CD. She couldn't place the reason, but the song had an extra feeling to it. She ran this by Jackie who agreed.

"You're right, Alana," she said after the song ended. "Gravitation Zero did have an extra feeling to it. Maybe the reason was because they used more emotion than they did on the CD."

"Maybe, I can't say what is different from the CD, but I can pick up something special about how Charlene sang and how Jesse, Karla, and Mark played. Now that I recall there is something special about this weekend in general. I just can't put my finger on it."

Alana thought to herself, *We should be able to put our whole hand on it. I can't quite understand it, but I can somehow detect that something even more extraordinary is going to happen this week.*

The girls finally waved good-bye to everyone as Mr. Shannonson had to leave to get back home. Alana still thought about the song, and the weekend and she wouldn't stop thinking until she figured out the mystery. Luck wouldn't help much to solve this case.

Catfight Crisis

Dear Alana,

I have been in a catfight with one of my friends for years. It started when she turned on me right out of the blue. Now she is not well liked by many people because she did the same to all of them. I want to know what is up with that.
--Tabby

Dear Tabby,

This person might have been having trouble outside of school or with her parents. That still gives her no right to pick on you. There will be people like the one you are dealing with so try to avoid her as much as possible. If you are seated near her in class, ask the teacher to move your seat. Don't deal with her and she won't deal with you.--Alana ☺

Alana and Jackie were in the back seat of Mr. Shannonson's dark blue Porsche. The only sounds that could be heard was the soft hum of the car on the road and the three of them breathing.

"Alana, Jackie would you mind if I stopped at your school to return the field trip approval form to Ms. Limner? Mr. Shannonson asked. "It was due on Friday and she said she would be in the classroom grading papers and preparing a display. I also want to speak with her about your progress."

"No we don't mind," replied Jackie.

"We'll be in the computer room next door working on the advice letters," continued Alana.

"I'm glad that you are so agreeable and so easy to deal with."

"Dad, I know you are planning a wisecrack, so are you?"

"You caught me! If you weren't so smart you'd be easier to fool." Mr. Shannonson laughed while Alana rolled her eyes.

He parked the car near the front entrance. After getting permission from the front office, Mr. Shannonson followed Alana and Jackie inside who raced to the computer room while Mr. Shannonson strolled into the room next door.

*   *   *

"Well, here is the place where we make our brilliant school newspaper," reported Jackie.

"You sound like a tour guide. To most people there's not a single thing appealing in our school, but to me it seems so big and deserted and waiting to be used again," responded Alana.

She and Jackie turned on some computers and waited for the programs to load. The only sound for a while was the speedy clicking of the mouse and swift clacking of the keyboard. Alana and Jackie were even enjoying themselves, that is, until Jane Luklit cruised into the room. Her face showed a look of utter disgust on her overly made-up face. As predicted earlier, Jane was wearing the same bandana that Jackie had worn at the video shoot.

"What the heck are you two doing here? Don't you know that this room is off-limits?" stomped Jane.

"If it's off limits then what are you doing standing in the middle of it?" Alana retorted.

"Special privileges, and I have this week's edition to finish. I don't see you with any pass!"

"We don't need a pass!" Jackie responded. "If we have work to do and there's an adult within one room away we can work here any time."

"Also we got permission from the office," Alana added.

"I'm going to need proof before I believe you."

...*And before you stop nagging us,* thought Alana, really annoyed.

"Ms. Limner and Mr. Shannonson are next door," said Jackie. "I repeat. We don't need a pass."

"If you're going to work, I'd suggest starting ASAP because the teachers aren't going to be here long." Alana suggested, trying to maintain her cool. If Jane would only stop nagging for just a few minutes, then being in the same building with her would be bearable.

Unfortunately Jane continued her probing. By the tone in her snobby voice, Alana could tell she was only getting started. Jane wasn't the least bit interested in what Alana and Jackie were doing, but if she could find a way to get the two them suspended or at least a few detentions, she would nose her way in their business. Alana was unlucky enough to get a whiff of the cosmetics Jane was wearing. She was desperate for oxygen.

Don't worry you'll be able to breath normally by summer vacation or at least by next month. It will all be over soon. It will all be over soon! Alana played these thoughts over and over again in her mind. She was doing her very best to ignore the trash talk Jane was throwingat her. She knew that her ears wouldn't be able to take in much more.

"Look, I am simply saying that you have no right to even be in this building unless you have a good explanation."

"OK! My dad is talking to Ms. Limner and submitting my travel forms for the field trip. My reason is that this is the last place I'd expect you to be." Alana normally wouldn't snap at anyone but at that moment she was steaming like Ol' Faithful. She finally lost her temper.

"Watch it Shannonson, you are as lucky as heck to even be on the school newspaper let alone that lowly advice column. If you aren't careful you could end up fired, demoted, in detention or..."

"...Next to you and your malevolent make-up for another breathless minute?" quipped Alana.

"Oh you are on thin ice now girl. Hope you are satisfied? We'll see what happens when school starts tomorrow. I have plans you know, big plans!" With that Jane strolled out of the room. She had an evil grin that reminded Alana of a jack-O-lantern. An evil scheme was cooking in Jane's mind. When Jane left, Alana felt that her lungs welcomed the fresh oxygen she and Jackie were now able to breathe.

"She really might be plotting revenge!" Jackie warned. "You can never tell. She most definitely is up to something. You should lock your locker and windows."

"I do lock my locker so nobody can steal anything or prank me. Look she's always hated me and other girls in school. Jane's been this way ever since I met her but she never did anything harmful to anyone who rubbed her the wrong way before. It's not like she'll break in through my bedroom window and strangle me. Since she thinks that she's such a goody two-heels she'd know that she'd get caught somewhere down the line. It's too risky for her reputation of little miss sweetheart to do something and have everybody know."

"Something about what she said convinced me that this time is different." offered Jackie.

"I've got you on my side, but I do wish I had my necklace. I always was comforted by that stone." Alana reached for the spot on her neck where her jade-stoned necklace hung. She remembered how it sparkled in the light and how she loved to look at it in the mornings. She felt a bit sad.

"You're right Alana, we'll always be there for each other. It takes more than one silly person to ruin a day."

"I'm not afraid of her, that *#@^*#... (Alana referred to Jane as something Jackie knew she wouldn't have even thought to say if school was in session!) I'd like to see her try to do her worst."

A New Friend

Dear Alana,

I am new at school and I want to fit in with the other jocks because they have similar interests as me. Unfortunately the only sport they play outside is football and that's the only one sport I don't play. Can I get some tips on how to fit in?
-Rejockted

Dear Rejockted,

Everyone was new to a school at some point so it is difficult for everyone to fit in. If you're a good athlete you can learn football at home or you can join a sport outside of football. Football won't be a sport all the guys play so you can also be introduced to the guys who play the sports you are good at. --Alana ☺

As the girls continued typing, a young girl about a grade younger than Alana and Jackie came in. She had dark skin, curly dark brown hair and was carrying a few heavy-looking textbooks and some stuffed folders.

"Is anyone else working here or may I join?" Her voice shook a little bit.

"Sure, you can, if you want," replied Jackie casually. She turned back to Alana and said, "Jane could be planning something really nasty. We don't know what she thinks but we do know her personality and heart. Both of which are colder than a winter of dry ice."

The young girl turned around and said, "Jane? Do you mean the brunette with the angry expressions and stinky make-up?"

"Yes, and I'm glad someone else agrees about the smell. How do you know her?" asked Alana.

"I'm the secret sports reporter for our school newspaper, Barbara Clark. I know that you are Alana, the advice columnist and this must be your friend, Jackie, who is the person who prints notices of all of the school events. Jane is the editor-in-chief, as she tells us at every meeting."

So Barbara was the secret sports reporter. No one was supposed to know who the sports reporter was. That way the school paper could cover the various events and give honest opinions about the games or matches with no spin from the coaches and players.

"Did you see her planning something in the hallway?"

"She was talking to herself, but I couldn't understand what she was saying because she was mumbling. I came here because I don't want her snapping at me like she came close to doing or what she does to you."

"She is hard to adjust to sometimes," admitted Jackie, who was ignoring the wicked grin on Alana's face that said, *you think?*

"Yes, I moved here the day before they had sign ups for after-school clubs and I didn't know many people that well."

"Well you can hang out with us," offered Alana. "Jane won't pick on you as much as she bullies us. The best thing to do is really ignore her no matter how much she mud slings."

Barbara put her books down and set the folders on top. Her arms seemed weary from lugging them everywhere. She switched on a computer next to Jackie, who peeked at her many books.

"You're taking a lot of courses," she remarked. "I don't mean to be nosy."

"It's okay. You can look. There's nothing personal in that pile."

"Oooh I didn't know they made Cow Daze folders and other school supplies. That's mine and Alana's favorite TV show!" squealed Jackie, making Alana jump in surprise.

"Yes, my uncle, Steven Charles, orders them in advance. But I don't mean to brag or anything. These materials won't appear for at least another month," answered Barbara.

"Wait. Hold on a second. Steven Charles is your uncle?" The clicking suddenly stopped from Alana's computer as she turned around for the first time.

"Why yes he is. I sometimes visit the studio and set. You can come sometimes if you'd like," responded Barbara.

"My dad works for him and we've been to the set a few times, but I've never seen you there," Alana said. She knew some things about Mr. Charles like he had a sense of humor, but she had no idea that he had some child relatives.

"You know, I thought I saw you, but I thought you were with Jane since you were talking with her so much that I didn't say hi. I should have recognized from the conversation you were having that you were not too happy with Jane. On the other hand, I did see her outside and she was yelling a lot at some boy she was with, but I don't really want to gossip. I was afraid she would get in my case. I am not too confrontational or aggressive."

"On your case," corrected Jackie.

"That's fine about wanting to keep a low profile," Alana added, "and I don't blame you, but don't you think you could be a little more outgoing and come a bit more out of your shell," suggested Alana.

"It might be better if you stand up for yourself. Don't be rude, but make sure you let people know that they can't bully you. Usually the person will back off. If that doesn't work, go to a teacher, your parents or the school guidance counselor. If you try being yourself, people will accept that."

"Wow! You really were meant to do an advice column."

"Actually I received an email from someone with a similar case. I remembered most of what I said to them. Right now I'm blanking and can't think of the advice I gave, but I usually do. I seem to have writer's block or something and I just can't think straight." Jackie rolled her eyes at Alana's comments.

She doesn't get it does she? Jackie thought to herself.

At that moment Mr. Shannonson opened the door to the computer room. "Alana, Jackie, we have to leave now."

"Bye Barbara, It was nice to meet you," called Jackie while she flipped off the computer switch.

"I'll see you at school tomorrow," added Alana as she shut down her computer.

"OK, bye!"

"Alana and Jackie decided to stop at their lockers. There was a note taped to Alana's locker. It read,

```
      I have plans for you tomorrow!
     You will regret everything you did.
```

Narrow Escape Escapade

Dear Alana,

    Its summer right now but when the season changes again I won't be able to ignore the fact that I'll need new clothes. My family can't really afford them right now, since I'm growing all of my clothes are passed down to my little sister. I don't want anyone to know but others are getting suspicious that we have no money. -Cashew

Dear Cashew,

    You can try going to bargain stores or thrift shops. They all have great prices. If you have a good friend in a larger size and (he or she) has things that no longer fit perhaps you can ask for them (for your sister and you). You can also take some fabric and make something yourself. Sometimes second-hand is better than extremely expensive or perhaps you'll find that you have talent and are able to make clothes for yourself. I do it and its fun. --Alana ☺

Alana woke up early on Monday morning. Although she wasn't the least bit worried about Jane's note she kept her eyes peeled when she was at school. Jackie had warned her to be extra cautious, even more than usual. Alana found nothing out of the ordinary as she checked everything twice and locked her locker between classes. She didn't even leave a scrap behind to ensure that she was safe from any trick Jane might attempt.

Alana felt relieved when lunch rolled around at 11:30. She bought her lunch, Mac-and-cheese, a speckled, ripe banana, and a slice of her favorite dessert, apple pie with whipped cream, topped with red sprinkles. She asked Jackie to keep watch while she got up to get a drink from the water fountain. Alana knew she believed that her arch rival was planning to strike, but she didn't want to give Jane the satisfaction by showing concern about the potential for revenge.

When Alana got back to the table she could see not too far away Jane in a crowd of seventh graders. Jane kept looking over towards Alana and smirking. Jackie didn't see anything unusual, but Alana kept careful watch. There was something unnervy about the way she was being stared at by Jane. If Jane wanted a reaction from her she wasn't going to get it. Jane kept peering at Alana, who ignored her completely. Jane had her own food so she didn't have any reason to even look at Alana's plate. Alana ate some more of her Mac-and-cheese which tasted reasonably good considering it was from the cafateria. Strange, good food in the cafeteria was highly unusual. Was that Jane's big plot? Did she plan to serve the entire grade tasty and delicious food in the cafeteria to weaken their resolve?

Alana finished her Mac-and-cheese quickly. She noticed Jane staring at the banana and apple pie slice that remained on the tray. Alana shifted her eyes away from Jane's hawk-eyed gaze and thought,

There's no way she's getting to my food. I won't let her have my favorite dessert, never in a million years is she going to get anything from me without either me putting up a fight or spiking it first with...

Alana took a closer look at her banana and apple pie slice. She was sure Jane was up to something. Alana looked again at her food and sniffed. She took one of the "sprinkles" between her fingers. The red speckles on the whipped cream appeared to have a strong odor and did not look like regular sprinkles. Alana recognized what it was. It was hot pepper seasoning, which could be found in any supermarket. Alana used her fork to investigate the slice of pie further. Sure enough, the apples had been stuffed with hot peppers and packed with spicy hot tamale sauce. She pointed this out to Jackie who only shrugged.

"She was planning something all along. This could be only the beginning. At least you caught on to the scheme in time," Jackie said.

"It's common sense and a bit of luck," replied Alana. "This can't be the end of her scheming, you do realize that, don't you?"

"Yeah, but I hope she gets kicked off the paper for this." Alana looked over at Jane who looked like she was swearing to herself as Alana threw out the dish. Alana could just imagine what Jane was thinking. Rats! She had failed her practical joke. Jane walked just behind Alana and Jackie on their way back to class from the cafeteria.

"You succeeded in embarrassing yourself and you failed in your little joke. You can lay off at any time," Alana declared.

"You're kidding! I'm just getting this soirée started," Jane retorted as she tossed back her hair with a mix of triumph and disappointment.

"Knock it off Jane. Alana doesn't deserve this treatment. Not even you would deserve to be poisoned like that," responded Jackie coolly.

"Well, you haven't seen the last or the worst I can do. I'd be way better at getting back at you if I wasn't at school where it's too distracting." With that Jane sashayed to her locker at the end of the corridor while Alana and Jackie turned down a separate hallway to reach their lockers. Alana found another hand written note taped to her locker door that read:

```
         I said this before,
        but I'll repeat it.
    This is only the beginning.
          You will be sorry!
     This battle will end with
      the right side victorious.
```

Alana ignored the note completely as she stuffed it in her backpack with the other one.

The Trip was Cancelled Due to Fog

Dear Alana,
*   One of my friends is clingy. She always follows me like a lost puppy to my locker even though hers is across the hall. I befriended her because she seemed pretty nice and she doesn't have many friends of her own. I've tried to ask her for some space but it never works. -Puppy trainer*

Dear Puppy,
* This person is clingy probably because she doesn't want to lose you as a friend. Since she doesn't have many friends maybe you should introduce her to some more of your friends. Maybe then she might stop relying on only you for attention. --Alana ☺*

"Alana this is getting out of control," mumbled Jackie.

"I've got plans for her too," responded Alana tossing the threatening letter into her backpack. She tried to dodge the knotted mob of seventh and eighth graders and still talk to Jackie. Alana made sure everything in her locker was well guarded.

"Well this is the second to last class I have with her until the three of us work tomorrow on the newspaper."

"Well, we were good at catching things like that poisoned pie prank so you should be alright." Jackie walked into the social studies room while Alana rushed off to science before the bell rang. After class Alana met up with Jackie again.

"She didn't try a single thing. Maybe she gave up?"

"She won't give up that easily. You can tell by the look on her face yesterday."

"Well, I know something's up and I will find out everything she's trying to pull off."

"Just keep your eyes peeled and expect the obvious."

Alana looked around the hallway. She saw a large fan in the hall. The school had no air conditioning so on a hot day a cooling fan was a welcome addition.

"Look what the school has added," said Alana.

"I noticed some other fans so this must be a change the school board voted for. There was a giant fan perched on the right side of the hallway with a cord running into the janitor's room. The cord was sitting loose on the ground. The fan was blowing crisp cool air and Alana felt as if she had just stepped through an air shower.

This cord on the floor is dangerous, thought Alana.

She remembers what Jackie had said, expect the obvious! Could this cord really be left by the janitor so dangerous like that on the floor? Alana walked over the cord just as it tightened. As it loosened again, Alana and Jackie shut the closet door, then strolled away from the cord and into a classroom.

"Another one of Jane's dirty tricks and another failure!" muttered Alana. The two girls heard the banging on the closet door as they sat in their seats.

"Gee do you think someone was hiding in that broom closet?" asked Jackie sarcastically.

"I don't want to jump to conclusions just yet. I don't have any real proof that anyone did anything," smiled Alana.

"It's too much of a coincidence for me to believe that the cord could simply lift itself up and down," replied Jackie, also smiling.

"When someone lets her out, she will surely make another attempt...something big to finish off the day. This is the second time she has tried to pull a prank and she always makes three tries. If you can evade that last one you'll probably be safe for good."

"I am almost certain I can avoid it. She can be pretty subtle, but Jane rarely does something that is too difficult to spot."

"We'll have to be on our toes." Jackie noted. Jackie saw a determined look on Alana's face that said that she wasn't about to give in.

The Final Straw

Dear Alana,

I am a few pounds overweight and want to get rid of the excess baggage. I'm not that sporty and I try to eat right. There are always treats in the house and I can't resist pigging out. I want to lose that extra weight before I turn obese. What should I do? -P.I.E turned P.I.G.

Dear Pie,

You don't have to be sporty to get the right exercise. You can take a nature hike or walk along your street and take pictures so it's not boring. Try asking your parents to hide the extra snacks so you aren't tempted. You also want plenty of rest and you could count how many calories you eat by reading nutrition facts. Whatever you do DON'T EVER SKIP MEALS! That will make you sick and you won't have any energy to do your work so you'll get bad grades and eventually you'll get too weak to do anything. Eat the right meals and don't be temped to eat unhealthy foods. Try to cut down on fast food also because the grease will just make you fat and/or sick. If you must eat how about celery or carrots. They are good and good for you. --Alana ☺

At 3:15 all the staff on the school newspaper gathered in the computer lab. Alana and Jackie got there a few minutes late because Ms. Limner simply had to make a tedious announcement about the following week's assignments and projects. She gave the class three handouts. So Alana and Jackie took extra time to put everything away.

When the two girls arrived, the computer teacher was out of the room. Naturally, Jane as the editor, was in charge. Alana took out some scrap paper to jot down any notes. She saw two free computers near where Barbara was working, so Alana figured that she should be as far from Jane as possible. Alana motioned for Jackie to follow. Unfortunately, before she reached the chair Jane caught on and she barked at Alana.

"You have to work where you normally do, Alana."

"Why, other kids are working in different places?"

"That's doesn't matter and besides I'm planning on using that computer today."

So you're actually going to apply yourself and even work today instead of yelling, and ordering everyone around? That's not the Jane Luklit I know and despise, thought Alana.

"The computer room has many extra computers so it won't make much of a difference."

"No protests! There's a deadline you know."

"No need to remind me. I remember the deadlines too, OK!" Rather than continue to argue with her, Alana just decided to let it go and sit in the chair that Jane wanted her to use.

"Just hurry up, sit down and let's get to work, Ms. Shannonson," growled Jane.

"I will!" Alana read the look on Jackie's face. It screamed, *just try and make me shut up.* Alana waved to Barbara as she put her things down under the seat.

"Hurry up and sit down already!"

"I don't see any reason to work so fast. Parts of my column were finished yesterday."

"You never know!" Jane looked pleased with herself at that remark, but Alana just ignored it. She switched on her computer, bent down to adjust the screen, she slid her chair out far enough, sat down and...

CRASH!!!!!!!!!!!!!!!!!!

Jane had succeeded in her practical joke this time, Alana's chair collapsed the second she sat on it, as she fell she bumped her head on the desk.

Alana's papers scattered all around the desk as she landed hard on her back on the concrete floor. Some people snickered, others looked worried, and Jackie ran over and asked Alana if she was OK.

"I'm fine!" she muttered, somewhat humiliated rubbing her head. Alana glared at Jane with an icy cold stare. At that moment she fell more anger at Jane Luklit than pain. She took a seat between Barbara and Jackie, both of whom wondered if she was all right.

Jane walked away with a wide grin on her face.

*   *   *

"She could get suspended for destroying school property," Jackie offered. Everyone had left the computer lab except Jackie, Barbara. and Alana (whose head was still throbbing from the fall).

"I can't believe she had the nerve to screw up the chair. Knowing her she wouldn't risk getting caught," Barbara added, as she picked up her books. Jackie remembered that she had forgotten a textbook in her locker. As the three stopped at Jackie's locker Alana found another note:

> You really deserved that little fall!
> I warned you that you would regret
> everything. The battle has ended
> with the good side having the victory.
>
> PS. Lose a few pounds before coming back!
> We don't want anymore broken chairs!

That was the final straw. Jane had gone over the edge and Alana knew exactly what to do.

Sweet Surprise For An All Day Sucker

Dear Alana,

I want to be a writer when I grow up but I'm getting my worst grades in my English class. I don't know why, but it just seems so difficult. I can write well at home, but in the class I can't string two words together that make a necklace, much less a sentence! -Needs a Miracle

Dear Miracle,

School may seem like it's tough but you will get deadlines and difficult assignments all throughout your life. Why don't you write an essay at home and show it to your teacher. Your teacher knows you can do well and writing is much easier when you have something to say. If you just look at the last sentence in your letter, you and many others will know that you are a great writer. At school make sure you have something to say when you write. -Alana ☺

P.S. Your (word necklace) might come in handy. I know mine once did.

Alana spent the next few hours brainstorming about what to do. She wanted to do something that wouldn't get her in trouble, but fun enough to get back at Jane. She knew it couldn't be bad, and she remembered what her dad had said to her when she was a little girl.

"Girls are vicious! Boys are idiots!"

Boy, he couldn't be more on target. Jane seemed to be the cruelest and nastiest girl that anyone could ever regrettably meet. Why was Sean stupid enough to still be talking to her, let alone hanging out with her?

Alana had heard Jane telling another girl, who looked fine, to lose weight. Telling someone to lose weight is just plain mean. It could cause the person to develop an eating disorder. Eating disorders could lead to serious health issues or even to death. Comments like that can lower the self-esteem of someone who would have otherwise been just fine with their appearance. No one should really care about someone else's weight unless that person is really has a medical need to lose it. Young girls can be crushed by such a nasty comment from someone who really has no right to interfere at all. That was simply just downright brutal. Alana thought she was starting to sound like a philosopher and a therapist, but it was true.

Alana could see that revenge would just aggravate Jane more and maybe make things worse, but she wanted something small to happen to make up for all the damage Jane did. She twirled her hair and wished she could twiddle with her lucky necklace. The jade stone always seemed to sparkle more when she thought.

I promised she wouldn't get to me but this time she just pushed me over the brink! Alana had to constantly remind herself to calm down. There had to be a loophole somewhere, somehow. Alana recalled everything that happened the past 24 hours from Jane's planning the prank to Alana falling hard on her back. Alana looked over the notes that Jane had left behind.

Alana called Jackie, who replied, "Nobody deserves what she did to you but you shouldn't get so mad about it. Everyone at school knows she is very obnoxious and very cruel, but retaliating won't solve a thing."

Alana knew Jackie was saying this to calm her down and it did work a bit. Jackie had said something Alana would usually say because she had asked her to help with the advice column. Alana was still fuming and she just had to get her anger out. She refused to be violent about it and talking about it just wasn't doing the trick. There had to be a solution to the whole "Jane" problem somehow.

"OK, I won't do anything like she did to me, but I will do something." Alana hung up the phone and for the next half hour she brainstormed until she came up with a simple yet brilliant idea.

Perfect! She muttered to herself. *Jane will never see it coming.*

Alana Strikes Back

Dear Alana,

I'm extremely annoyed with one of my friends for telling one of my secrets and I want revenge. I don't want to be too vengeful but I need to get this extra anger energy out of my body. -Power

Dear Power,

It's not a good idea to jump to conclusions. If you want the extra energy gone you can scream into a pillow and punch it. Don't do anything to any person and try to keep you secrets to yourself from now on -Alana ☺

Early the next morning, Alana gathered every scrap of paper she needed. If she was going to pull this off she needed to be convincing. She was too excited to eat her breakfast of waffles and fruit. When both her parents were ready to leave, her dad drove her to school so she got there earlier than the buses.

"I didn't know it was 2012 already!" Mr. Shannonson joked "Shouldn't I be driving you to Josh Breddles High School?"

"I don't need that much sleep! If I did I'd be fifty!"

"Have a good day!"

"I will."

Alana raced to the office, where she gave them a note and received another to deliver. Then she cruised upstairs to the lockers where she brought the message and put it in one of the lockers, and went off to her homeroom class. Alana could use the time to study for the upcoming tests and finals.

When the buses arrived, the silence in the school was broken by crowds of seventh and eighth graders noisily going to their lockers, and then rushing off to their homerooms before the morning bell. Alana wondered when her message would be received.

When she saw Jackie and Barbara she clued them in with what was about to happen.

"Well, maybe someone who works at school will finally realize that she is really the devil in cosmetics," replied Jackie.

"Look! Jane found the note in her locker," commented Barbara. Jane had come in late that morning.

"She probably got herself a fresh manicure on the other side of town. She definitely smells like acid," scowled Alana. "And, I wish she was still there."

Jane dialed her lock combination as she set her full backpack on the floor. When Jane opened up her locker she found a small note.

**Please see me in the office at
lunch time! We need to discuss
something important!
From Mrs. Belling!**

"Simple, yet effective," whispered Alana. "I'll explain later."

*   *   *

"What exactly did you do and how exactly is Mrs. Belling, our principal, helping?" asked Jackie.

"Did you see that Jane wasn't in the cafeteria today?" responded Alana.

"Yes, but what does that have to do with…"

"You know Jane had been trying to get me with nasty pranks like spiking my food and damaging chairs for 'quote unquote' "making fun of her." Mrs. Belling knew that someone was vandalizing the school's property. Jane thought that I would have no proof that she did anything against anything or anyone. But she forgot one thing. She forgot completely about…"

"What, about what?" asked Jackie.

"…the evidence. Those cute little threats she composed and put in my locker. Mrs. Belling would probably know everyone's handwriting because like any principal she visits every classroom. I'm absolutely positive that she knows Jane and me well enough to know who will tell the truth and who the story teller is. It's almost like one of those murder mystery shows on TV."

"Then why were you putting a note into her locker?"

"Jane's mother called the school yesterday saying Jane would be late today. I overheard that important piece of information from Mrs. Belling while I was at the office this morning. Jane had a dentist appointment, but her new scent also says that she stopped at the nail salon afterwards without permission. Mrs. Belling knows that Jane was cutting class, since her mom said when she was supposed to be done at the dentist. Also Mrs. Belling knew that I got hurt when the chair was damaged in the school paper office yesterday. She was mad and asked me about the chair incident. I don't know for sure who damaged the chair, but I showed the threatening notes to Mrs. Belling.

Mrs. Belling didn't want a lot of people to know Jane was cutting class or was possibly damaging school property. So she wrote the note, and the secretaries knew that I had classes with Jane. So when Mrs. Belling wrote out the note I was asked to drop it into Jane's locker. Jane did two things wrong. She was cutting class and damaging school property."

"Not to mention hurting you." said Jackie and Barbara.

"You got back at Jane. I can't believe you pulled that off so quickly and easily without being mean. It didn't even take that long to explain."

"Elementary Jackie. Jane will get a detention or even more for her pranks, so she will be doing "hard time" after school, which also means that she can't be here at the Walk Street Journal offices to rant at me, or otherwise I'd be deaf by now." Alana tried her best to sound like the famous detective Joe Friday from the 1950's cop show *Dragnet*, the one her grand parents watched at their house on weekends.

"News of this catfight event will spread around fast," stated Jackie, as she looked around the cafeteria and the area where the other seventh graders were running around.

"News doesn't pass through this building like an ego-maniac in a mirror shop or a candy lover on Halloween night, it goes around quickly." Alana giggled, she loved Jackie's unique comparisons. Jackie always managed to have her pronouncements make sense. When she heard the words candy lover, Alana imagined a giant Hershey bar as big as James Walk Middle School with the entire school chewing away. Suddenly a tinny bell echoed throughout the school.

"Awww man, the one time we can talk without getting told off by a teacher we only have a limited time, and we can't finish what we wanted to say," moaned Jackie.

"Hey don't worry, we can still talk after school while working on the school newspaper for tomorrow's edition, or while we have free time between classes," Alana responded.

"By the way, the newspaper today with our articles was a hit. I wish my advice was better though." Alana looked over at a small crowd of girls and guys nearby reading the newspaper. Some were giggling at the comics that were included in it every day.

Jackie rolled her eyes.

A Sweet Silent Session

Dear Alana,

I am extremely forgetful and I can't remember what I want to say to my friends. As a result I chatter non-stop in class. My teachers have warned me that if I talk with my friends just one more time I'll get a detention.
-Chatter Squirrel

Dear Squirrel,

Why don't you write down what you are going to say in advance, so you won't bother anyone during classes. Keep track of what you say before you say it so your conversation will be shorter and you'll be more on task in class. -Alana ☺

After class, Jackie and Alana walked down the corridor to the computer lab expecting to hear rants and raves for being late once again. As they entered the room they were astonished to hear only an occasional whisper while almost everyone else was silent.

"Wow it's quieter in here than a teenager's dinner conversation," Jackie whispered. Jane was apparently not attending the Walk Street Journal reporter's meeting that afternoon. Alana was pleased about that. She knew that she wouldn't have to worry at all about Jane's criticizing insults, or Jane overworking her, or any of the other usual noise caused by the editor-in-chief. Alana clued Barbara in to the details of the earlier incident. Barbara was as amazed as Jackie was.

"Wow what a story. I thought you were being very secretive and acting like a detective lately."

"Thanks! I'll give you more of the scoop later but I've got to get to work on my column or I'll miss the deadline," Alana replied.

Barbara turned back to her sports screen while Alana looked at the clock over the front door. It read 3:10. Alana knew she should start working, but something had caught her attention out of the corner of her eye. Sean had turned around to see what was going on. He saw Alana and waved to her. There was a little bit of concern on his face. She waved back and both turned around. Perhaps he hadn't forgotten about Alana falling from her chair yesterday. Jane made him deputy editor-in-chief and Alana suspected it was to catch her if she talked with her friends. Either way Alana was eager to start her column now that she had the proper motivation. She read the first letter in her pile.

> *Dear Alana,*
>
> *My friend, Valerie, keeps ignoring me at school. She is in a big clique and is always spending time with the other girls. The girls in her clique are kind to me but I don't really like being in a big crowd. When we are not at school she spends more time with me. I do have other friends but they aren't in any of my classes this year like Valerie is and I don't see her as often as I would like to. Is there a way I can spend more time at school with her and if so, how? -Neglected*

This seemed like a pretty easy letter to answer. Alana responded,

> *Dear Neglected,*
>
> *There is another way you can spend more time with Valerie. Try asking her to sit with you at lunch to just be with you once in a while. Get her alone and tell her how you feel. If she is a true friend she'll understand. It's great that you have other friends so you don't have to rely on only her. Try to become friendly with some of the other girls that she hangs out with. If they happen to be in any of your classes you might end up not feeling like a loner most of the time. Sincerely,*
>
> *Alana a.k.a. Candy Apple*

Alana could answer only one more letter for her column so there would be enough room for the rest of the articles. She was at her limit. She read the next letter silently to herself.

Dear Alana,

I really like this person who is in many of my classes. He is always hanging out with buddies so I never get to talk to him. He has been looking at me a little bit with a little smile so I think he's interested. This girl who annoys him keeps asking if he likes other girls in our grade and then his buddies tease him. I am a shy person so I don't really know the best approach because I really want to keep quiet about my secret. Is there any way I can talk to him without causing trouble. -Shy but Sweet

This letter was slightly more challenging than the last one, so Alana tried to answer as best as she could.

Dear Shy

You aren't the only one with a conflict like this. The best thing is the direct approach. If that doesn't work for you try sending a letter or an email. You can look up his address in the local phonebook. You can also ask one of his (more trustworthy) female friends what his email address is. Just ignore this annoying girl. Sometimes girls just want to cause trouble for laughs. Guys sometimes are the same way. You don't have to mention anything about your secret. If you feel the need to tell him at the right time just do it. Give yourself the confidence you need.

Sincerely,

Alana a.k.a. Candy Apple

Alana reread the letters to herself. They both seemed about right. She was about ready to print the letters when Sean walked up to her computer, and said, "If you want you can answer an extra letter for this week's edition. We have some spare space as the other articles are short. You still have time before we go to press." Sean pointed at the clock. He was right. There was about a half hour left before the final copy was needed.

"Thanks!" Alana smiled as Sean turned to go back to his seat. His blond hair waved as he walked. Alana couldn't help but notice that the clicking of keys in the computer had been continuous compared to the usual meetings where there was more talking than working going on. Sean had been helping the fifth and sixth graders that had been working in the computer lab (unlike Jane who disapproved almost every word written from all the younger kids). Since he let Alana answer an extra letter she opened up the last one she had received.

> *Dear Alana,*
>   *This pain in the neck person in one of my classes really gets on my nerves. She asks who I like in front of my friends. She just thinks of a girl out of the blue in other classes and asks if I like her. I can't answer because I do like a girl in the same class as the annoying one. The guys ask me about it later and then rib me if I don't answer or try to make up excuses to avoid the subject. I never know what to say. If the other guys ever find out the truth they'll never let me live it down. -Confused dude*

Alana reread this letter. She also looked back at the letter before. They had a similar connection. Two people in school like each other a lot. A girl in one of the classes they all have together annoys them both. The guy's friends will tease him and the girl is shy. This letter was the biggest stumper she had come across that day. After much thoughts Alana finally came up with a reply and slowly typed,

> *Dear Confused,*
>   *It's natural to like somebody as more than a friend. If you've known her for a long time tell her what you think about her. If you see her alone ask to speak with her. You don't have to worry about your friends. They aren't used to, or have never experienced the feeling you have so you don't have to be embarrassed. If they tease you for liking a girl they might just be jealous, immature or might just want some "guy-only" time. If you say something to the annoying girl or tell a teacher how much of a pain she is, she might stop bothering you. If you hang out with the girl you like as just friends you might find out that she likes you too.*
> *Sincerely,*
>
> *Alana a.k.a. Candy Apple*

94

Alana looked over the responses she had written. Everything looked in order. She gazed up at the clock. There were still fifteen minutes left of the meeting. Alana printed out her work and gave it to the messenger who collected everything to be sent down to the printing room. Someone asked what they should do next.

Sean offered, "Either you could work on the next day's newspaper, play computer games, or leave early."

Cheers erupted from all of the fifth graders and sixth graders. The boys grouped together to play some new games on a popular website while the girls started on homework. The two eighth grade girls who were on the committee left the room chatting about their plans when they got back to their homes. There were about six seventh graders from one homeroom, who were on the newspaper team altogether, and they started to clean their desks. Two other seventh graders, boys joined the sixth graders on the website. Everyone seemed real happy. Jane never did show up. Sean, Alana and Jackie began packing up everything.

Alana and Jackie waved good-bye to Barbara, who smiled back, but she had her head bent over her computer to finish her assignment by the deadline. There was a mob of fifth graders in the hall. Some looked like they were very busy because they rushed down the stairs to greet their parents outside. Others explored the school around them. They were curious to see what the corridors that were in looked like because one day they would be there.

"Let's see if your dad has showed up yet," Jackie suggested. "He usually arrives ahead of time."

"All right, let's take the shortcut so we can see which direction he's coming from."

The two teens walked to the parking lot and saw Mr. Shannonson just outside the door. He waved to them.

"Hey Alana, hello Jackie, how's the career going?"

"Journalism let us out early today," Alana responded

"Jane wasn't there and everyone finished everything on time so Sean let us out in advance," Jackie finished.

"Why would the boss miss a council meeting?"

"Dad, this is the school newspaper not a business. Today, we worked as fast as a cheetah during the mile run."

"What's a mile run?" inquired Mr. Shannonson.

"That's when we run a mile around the field for a physical fitness test. It's required by the state." Alana made sure her dad didn't miss the sarcastic tone.

"I didn't know a mile could run," replied Mr. Shannonson.

"Real weak, dad," replied Alana.

"You really like to joke around Mr. Shannonson, don't you?"

"Yes, I do Jackie, I've always loved a good gag so don't laugh too much when I make some of the famous Shannonson-style witty comments."

"No problem with that dad," Alana replied.

Mr. Shannonson laughed at Alana's wisecrack. He understood what she meant even though it was at his expense.

"I expect great things from my daughter. She come up with some great comebacks for sidesplitting laughter. Knowing you, Jackie, you're really good with puns as well."

"I've been working to improve my puns for about as long as ants have been working to get things into their hills. No simile intended." answered Jackie.

"Dad, maybe you should actually say something that's funny or make at least make little more sense, but at least your delivery is good,." Alana offered.

"I'm all ears, Alana."

"Yeah, like a carpenter is all thumbs."

Everyone got in the car wondering what would happen when Jane came back to the newsroom, but no one imagined what was actually going to happen.

The Cool Classics of Comedy

Dear Alana,

I'm a serious person but nobody understands that I can be funny also. When I try to make a joke only my best friends understand. I think I can tell some great jokes, but nobody seems to get what I mean. -Dry sense of humor

Dear Humor,

It's great that you want to be a funny person. If your friends are puzzled, perhaps you should explain what you mean. Humor is as much about delivery as it is about content. If you want to make jokes when you talk, you should be aware that you think is funny may not be funny to others. Use your humor wisely, some people will just never get it. -Alana ☺

Jackie lived farther away from the school than Alana did, so during the car ride Alana quizzed Jackie on her comparisons and puns to pass the time. She seemed to have one for almost every topic Alana threw at her. Some puns were humorous, others were serious, but all of them made at least some sense. Alana and Jackie felt that they could use a good laugh so that they would get rid of the serious, working, school mood they were in.

"Happiness."

"I'm felling joy like an oyster feels clammy."

"Bored."

"If this was any more uninteresting it would be used as somebody's project in wood shop."

"Brainstorming."

"When I give this thought my brain will be raining down a storm."

"Play on words."

"Why they'd be too small to see, let alone mess about on."

"Why does sea food has such a strong flavor?"

"Because the ocean if full of mussels!"

"Anger."

"Anger is like a fan. Both blow hard."

"What it feels like to be a dog."

"It feels ruff."

"What it feels like to be a smart cat."

"It's purr-fact!"

"How you feel right now?"

"I'm as confused as a guy in the girls' locker room." This comeback caused Alana to chortle a little bit.

"OK, I give up, you win!"

"I did like the one about the genius cat," chuckled Mr. Shannonson. "Are you sure we aren't related?"

"Jackie's flying solo on her comedy routine so you can't take any credit from her. Unlike her I'm related to you so I know what you think."

"Were you ever the class clown when you went to school, Mr. Shannonson?" Jackie asked with burning curiosity.

"Oh yes. I was the clown from first grade through my freshman year in College. After that we all were clowns. Steve Charles was my best friend back then and still is. Together we'd pull some major pranks on teachers, who wouldn't care. Every April fools day we'd try to break our previous year's record for pranks!"

"Dad, I didn't know Steven Charles went to school with you."

"Yes, we knew each other since we were five years old. We now talk about the jokes we used to pull and what our kids would do now if they follow in our footsteps."

"What sorts of pranks did you do?"

"We never did anything vengeful, violent or damaging. Steve was always the idea man and I was the daredevil. We would sometimes bring fake vomit in to school to try and get out of tests and quizzes. We'd slip whoopee cushions under couches in the library.

Once in fifth grade on the day when we brought pets in to school, this boy would boast and brag about how well-trained Oscar, his Doberman was. He'd make fun of our pets. When he put Oscar back in his cage and when every-one was taking a break, we'd put fake dog-doo at the back of the cage and add a little dirt. I would've added melted chocolate but Steve and I knew that it would be a big give-away as well as a waste. We were also famous for the choco-late we brought every day, but back to my story. When he came back, he was furious."

Alana and Jackie giggled. They had gotten out of their working mood, but they wanted to get ideas for fun pranks and Mr. Shannonson always told interesting stories.

"What other things did you do?" asked Jackie.

"Please tell us! Please, please!" begged Alana.

"All right. Well, we acted the silliest in elementary school but our best jokes were in middle school."

"Did you go to any school that we have gone to?"

"Not the elementary school Alana, but I did go to James Walk Middle School."

"Wow I didn't know our school was that ancient!"

"As I was saying, one of our best jokes was one we did to the school bully. His name was Bobby Ronninski and he was our main target. He had a bad reputation at school for being mean to kids in the lower grades, as well as a real egomaniac and a show-off. Our best wasn't the dog prank but Steve and I pulled off a lot of stunts on Bobby. Our personal favorite was in sixth grade.

Bobby was always showing off his neon sports jacket. Back when I was a kid, neon colors were a major fad. He would look down at everyone who didn't have something neon. He would call everyone ugly wildcats that belonged in the jungle. So we made a giant poster and put in on a wooden frame high in the Gym. In big letters we painted the message on the poster:

```
        Bobby Man, Do the school a massive favor
   and put on an different mask! The one you're already
   wearing isn't working well enough. The loud colors on
    your jacket scream that they belong to one ugly cat.
              Peace out from this ceiling.
    P.S. It would be groovy if you started shopping now!
```

"When the news spread around school, we were famous. Bobby, naturally threatened to beat us up, but we knew he could never take us on together or individually. That's the way it is with bullies really. He told the principal and we got punished by having to clap erasers for a week. Pop wasn't pleased at all. But the big man at home, my dad, couldn't hide the fact he was proud of his jester of a son who stood up to the bully. He still grounded me for a day. He believed that grounding for more than that was too harsh."

"That prank must've had a really great result," giggled Jackie.

"It had a hilarious effect. He stopped showing-off and quit bullying for good."

"Wow that feeling of victory must have felt good for a very long time," gawked Alana.

"It was sure fun and games for a while but at the end of the school year, Steve and I realized that what we had done was really mean, cruel and as Daffy Duck would say, "Deth-picable"".

Despite all the fun Steve and I had during the year, we realized that revenge isn't the best solution no matter how annoying a person is. We felt truly awful about every single stunt. When we played practical jokes and were tattled on, the two of us knew that we were being punished for a very good reason. When you tell a teacher on someone, it's very different than trying to handle the situation on your own."

Alana remembered that she too had longed to get revenge on Jane for making her chair collapse. She was glad she hadn't stooped down to Jane's level and caused an all out war.

"So what did you finally do?" she asked her dad. Alana was hoping for an idea to makeup for everything she did.

"Steve and I managed to convince each other that the best thing to do was to apologize. One day the two of us just walked up to Bobby and said how sorry we were to make fun of him. He thought that it was another trick. Once he realized that Steve and I weren't lying, he ended up becoming one of our best friends. In the end we acted as though the enmity between us never happened.

In high school, he actually introduced me to your mother because I was shy and having trouble talking to girls. If you think about it, if it wasn't for me making up for the damage I had caused, you wouldn't even have been born! Even saying sorry for a rude comment can effect your future in ways you cannot predict. I know this might not mean a lot to you right now but someday this advice will come in handy."

Mr. Shannonson parked his car in Jackie's driveway and she hopped out and waved good-bye. Alana thought right away that her dad's story made sense the very minute the words had left his lips. They went around and around inside Alana's head before plunging deeply into her heart.

I now know it's up to me to repair this mess. Alana thought to herself. *Captain Arben was right. I do always take time to come up with an answer. I'm more like dad than I ever thought.*

A Word Gained

Dear Alana,

There's this guy who always copies my homework. If I was paid a penny for every time he did it I could buy a mustang. I've tried moving my seat but he always finds a way of sitting near me. The only reason he's doing this is to impress a girl in class. I want my answers to be original.
-Different Dude

Dear Different,

Try to move away from him. I would not recommend writing some of the answers wrong and then when he looks away, quickly changing the answers to get them right. No you should not do that. However, when you hand in your work or answer the questions, tell the teacher what really happened or get this guy to admit what he did. He'll be mad, but cheating and plagiarism is about as bad as it gets.
-Alana ☺

For the first time in her memory, Alana Shannonson actually wanted to find Jane Luklit, her longtime arch rival. Jackie was dumbfounded when Alana gave Jackie her explanation during a free period.

"Look, dad didn't just make up that story for kicks. It meant something and it wasn't just for gags or stunts or to tease. My dad knows I try to be a good person and the guilt I'm feeling is like indigestion of my heart."

"Good comparison Alana, but it sounds corny. Well, good luck trying to find or get through to her. Jane's bound to be steamed after getting busted for what she did."

"That's her fault, not mine! The most complex part of all of this will be persuading her that I'm not lying."

"Nice knowing you!"

"That's what you said last year when you dared me to swallow a jalapeno pepper, even though you knew I hated spicy foods of any sort."

"But you instantly took the dare and did it simply by eating it faster and without even one complaint."

"Could we please get back to the topic of finding Jane?"

"She's not here today," piped up a small voice. Barbara Clark had overheard and now joined the conversation. She was on her way to her Spanish class on the second floor.

"What do you mean she's not here today?" Alana feared that she had caused that trouble as well.

"Well at least she's not here right now. I was recently transferred to a Spanish class up here."

Jane would normally be spotted or at least her smell would be in the corridor by this time because all the seventh graders have most of their classes there.

"You do have an excellent point there," Alana agreed.

"Are all sixth graders geniuses or just you?" Jackie asked.

"We do our homework more often and pay more attention than fifth graders and seventh graders. I just judge by what I hear when I'm in the hallways, so no offense."

"None taken."

"Is this the first time you transferred classes?"

"No, this is the second time I've transferred, but this school has a tougher curriculum than the last one I went to."

"You fit in perfectly here. At James Walk, the sixth and eighth graders are the smartest you'll find. Eighth graders study more for high school."

"What about fifth and seventh graders?" Alana asked. She was curious about what why or how Barbara knew this much.

"Fifth graders are still considered elementary schoolers so teachers don't really expect much from them, and the result is that the fifth graders take advantage of their last year as 'immature' students. I've also noticed that seventh graders like to have fun and enjoy themselves more than they study. This is mostly because they are more interested in their social status. Most would rather like to be considered more 'popular' than 'smart' because some are entering their teenage years, and they're positioning themselves for eighth grade."

"How did you discover all of this?" Jackie had become completely entranced with the conversation. Barbara's knowledge and powers of observation were amazing. It seemed she knew the middle school from the inside-out.

"People usually don't notice me standing around when they are talking. As a result, I observe the details of their interactions and when combined with other data leads me to a logical and often correct conclusion."

"It sounds like someone spends way too much time on practicing the scientific method," Alana teased.

"I think of observation as a memory experiment—a sort of mnemonic. There are a lot of facts to be gained by just looking and listening. Most things about behavior are directly under your noses right in front of you," replied Barbara.

"Are you going to be a scientist when you grow up?" Alana had no idea that understanding other kids was so visible to an unaided eye and that she could really see what was going on if she just looked around a bit.

"I honestly don't know. There are so many possibilities to choose from. Many careers will require a generously proportioned quantity of knowledge," replied Barbara.

Alana was now fully absorbed with this dialogue. All thoughts about Jane were driven clean out of her mind. She, like Barbara had never cared about popularity. Alana had never longed to be in a major clique, although sometimes she wouldn't have minded a small bit of extra attention every now and then. She always thought the whole idea was wild. Now, she realized the whole middle school 'process' was really one big, relationship building learning experience, but the diversity of other kids' personalities made it so difficult.

At that moment a familiar odor filled the corridor. Alana could place her finger on the scent exactly. Jane had arrived in school. Alana pointed out to Jackie and Barbara that the aroma seemed lighter and more acceptable than usual.

"Wish me luck," Alana whispered.

She tried to squeeze her lucky charm tightly, but caught her self in time. She had caused herself and her friends trouble, she thought to herself. She was going to make up for it and hopefully get the pressure off everyone's shoulders.

Alana's Dare

Dear Alana,

Everything I like to read is too easy for my reading level. I love the Nancy Drew series, but my parents refuse to get me any more because I should challenge my mind. I want to read mysteries and exciting novels but the new Harry Potter book doesn't come out until next year. How do I find a good book to read? -Empty Paige

Dear Empty,

Why don't you find your reading level before you choose a book? There will be many to choose from. Or you can step up to a higher level and choose one of the books your parents read. If there's something you don't understand, ask someone who knows or look it up yourself. You will get smarter this way. -Alana ☺

It took all the courage Alana possessed to walk up to her rival. Jane might make some nasty comments, try another practical joke, or she might even have a prepared plan just waiting for her. Alana knew she'd feel better if she fixed the damage. She wanted the guilt knife in her gut to vanish. What was she to say?

"Hi, Jane!" Not much of a start, but her at least it was something. Alana wished Jackie and Barbara weren't watching. If this went well, she'd prefer to tell them about it later than have them watch it live.

She grudgingly continued, but Jane said, "What is it?"

She didn't turn around and the tone in her voice suggested that she didn't want company. Alana suspected that she was still mad about her visit to Mrs. Belling's office.

"So I was wondering..." *Stop beating around the bush and get to the point already!* Said a loud voice ringing in Alana's head.

Voices always appeared like leprechauns when Alana found herself in a sticky situation. This voice was a wise guy and very sarcastic. Alana liked to keep her thoughts sweet. Other voices annoyed her, but sometimes they helped out a lot. She knew the prankster voice wasn't going to disappear so quickly.

Do you want to get this over with or not? said the voice in her head.

OK already. said another voice in Alana's head. Jane looked-up and appeared to finally listen.

"Look, I'm sorry about everything that happened. There's a lot going on right now and I didn't mean to take anything out on you."

Are you happy now? asked the first voice.

What do you think? Of course I'm happy. Just listen for the response. You'll know what to say after that. I hope you're right.

Jane turned around and to Alana's surprise, she looked very sincere and natural.

"Are you serious?" asked Jane.

"I would need fabric or skin hardener for my face if I wasn't, if there was such a thing."

"I probably should say the same. My parents are getting divorced and I won't see them happy together ever again. They are always both very busy with work, and I am not sure what is going to happen to me or with which parent I am going to live. They are fighting a lot. Since my dog, Skippy died, I've been pretty lonely. You and your friends have always had a family who loved you. You, Jackie, and Barbara never really considered me as a friend. That's why I've been more of a pain to you than to anyone. I really didn't mean to hurt you when I loosened a screw on your chair. I shouldn't have been so stubborn to try to get you to understand." Jane began to cry a bit.

"Jane, maybe it would be easier to talk to someone you trust."

"That's what I'm doing isn't it? Getting advice in person is a lot better than sending a letter to the advice column."

Alana didn't know how to respond. Jane was counting on her for some useful advice. She had to follow through.

"Jane, no one had any idea that your parents were going through a divorce or even about your dog. You always seem so strong, so tough. Have you spoken to the guidance counselors? They may be able to help your parent understand what you're going through" Alana felt her eyes moistening.

"I don't mean to sound mean, but we really should go to the girls room 'cause your tears are smearing your make-up. Maybe we should wash off all the make-up first. You'd really be much more beautiful without it."

Jane peered into her locker mirror. What looked back was a facade of rosy lips, dusted cheeks, painted eyes, and a very unhappy face.

"It's not the real you," Alana said gently.

Jane and Alana took five minutes in the girl's bathroom to wash off every bit of make-up Jane had on. Even Jackie and Barbara offered to help out. When Jane emerged the mascara was down the drain and her blue eyes were much more noticeable. Her cheeks were no longer dusted with powder, but softer looking and normal. For the first time ever, a genuine smile could be seen on her. Her white teeth gleamed. She appeared more beautiful with this natural look. Jane's mask was finally removed and locked away for good. She reached into her pocket and pulled out a small shiny object. It was Alana's missing necklace.

"I found this on the floor of the Cow Daze set after the concert," Jane said. "I'm sorry I held it for so long. Please take it."

Alana gently took the necklace and put it around her neck once again. It seemed that now all was right with the world, but since life never stands still, there would soon be more challenges for everyone to face.

To Show the World

Dear Alana,

I love the way I look but my parents don't like what I wear. They think it's too trashy. They are super strict and don't want me outdoors unless my shirts are half an inch from my neck and I have no holes in my jeans. How do I convince them that they need to relax and lighten up? -Turtle

Dear Turtle,

Most parents don't want their kids to grow up too fast. Parents want to keep their kids as young as they can. Sometimes they cross the line. Maybe if you get on their good side, they will lighten up about what you wear. It's always worth a try. -Alana ☺

Wow you really pulled something off! The small voice in Alana's head reappeared again.

I thought you'd be gone already. Alana's other voice replied.

Fat chance, you do realize you saved an entire school of shy kids from a century of catfights and you even saved me money on popcorn. The voice was convincing as well as being extremely annoying. Alana still wished it would disappear.

Don't let this go to your head!

I am in your head.

You know what I mean.

Barbara and Jackie both approved of Jane's new look.

"It looks so authentic and its way nicer than before."

"It's as convincing as..." Jackie couldn't think of anything to say. She was speechless. She just couldn't find any words to describe Jane's new look.

"Sean will love the new you," Alana said. Alana knew if Sean truly liked Jane he might as well enjoy the real her instead of the made up one. It lifted her personality up several notches.

"I don't think I can get close to a guy right now," responded Jane. "Besides, I always knew he liked you and you liked him back. I couldn't stop myself. Either way, he's all yours."

Score! Touchdown! However else you sports-fans express victory.

Are you going to be here much longer?

Maybe. I plan to stay a little bit longer. By little I mean forever more. I like being a prankster and I'm positive you will need me. You finally have the guy! I'll be here for advice when you lovebirds chit-chat.

Shut it you! Alana said to the voice in her head.

Why do I have to shut up? You forgot that I don't have a mouth, Ha!

Please, just lay low for a while.

Fine, but I get to explore your memories.

Not If I have anything to say about it!

Don't you mean think about it? Stupid little wise guy. Alana was relieved when she could no longer hear the wise-cracking smart voice in her head anymore so while Jackie flashed a grin, she turned to Jane.

"If you never liked Sean why did you hang out with him all the time?"

"To make you jealous, and because I did like him a little myself. I know that it's sappy and such but I was willing to do almost anything so I wouldn't be so lonely."

"Why didn't you make friends with other girls in the seventh grade?" asked Barbara.

"They all hate me because of how I acted. I thought I'd never be able to make up for that."

"Then what about girls in other grades?" Alana saw many other possibilities. She wasn't about to give up easily. "And it's never too late to take action to control what you did."

"We could each call you tonight so we could practice on what you should say to others," Jackie suggested.

"I never thought of that! Why can't we do it now?" Jane seemed so eager to expand her friendships with other girls.

112

When they were rivals Alana knew Jane wasn't willing to get better or even be told she needed to perk up. The bell over the intercom chimed three times to say that the free period for seventh graders was over.

"That's why!" laughed Alana.

Practice, Practice, Practice
Makes Perfect, Perfect, Perfect

Dear Alana,

I am going to start high school next year. I want to add some flair to my backpack because I'm forbidden to get a new one. How can I add the flair I want? -Sweet Stylez

Dear Stylez,

A simple accessory can go a long way. Try adding some awesome key chains. If that isn't enough, you should always try getting a bedazzler. They will add rhinestones and sparkle to whatever you put it on. Your style may even sell for a profit. -Alana ☺

That evening, Jackie and Barbara met in Alana's house. Alana borrowed her parent's cell phone and found the school phone book. While they looked up the number, the wise-cracking voice popped back in Alana's conscious.

Hey, rookie! Still trying to improve school?

I thought I told you to shut up. Jane is actually eager to be better than she was.

Actually I'm back from your daydream. I've been on vacation for the day.

Well stay put in my daydreams then.

Why bother, it's more entertaining here. Three reasons. One, you need me. Two, I help you with advice, but I like to goof off. And three, its fun annoying you and come up with jokes you might want to use. Sadly, I can't claim any credit.

Just put a brain cell in it.

And have you lost a valuable part of yourself? What about that pretty little necklace you always wear?"

That valuable part would be preferable to you.

Not a chance!

When her inner voice appeared as a wise guy or wise her-ess, Alana truly wished that it would go back to being part of her sweet side. Alana secretly blamed her dad for the voice in her head because she inherited her funny side from him.

Actually, the phone at Jane's house had already rung four times but there wasn't any answer. Nobody seemed to be at her home. The second time Alana dialed, the voice was still bouncing around her head, but she was able to ignore it, so maybe it really had taken a vacation. The phone rang another four times but still nobody answered.

"Maybe she's at her dad's place for the night before the divorce is final," suggested Barbara. She knew that Jane's parents were living apart.

"Or Jane could be at the place where her mom works," added Jackie. "It's only 5:30 so maybe she hasn't come home yet. She did say that she had to meet with her parent's lawyers in their office or at her Uncle's."

"Well, Jane should know my email address. Let's check the home computer." The three girls raced across the hallway to check the computer.

Once again, Alana's head started talking to her.

Before I go on to my next voyage from Arben Harbor, remember not to rush to conclusions about someone just the same way you and your friends just rushed over to the computer.

Just scat to the harbor and take your sweet time. How can I miss you if you won't go away?

You read way too many joke books.

My definition of "adult's only" means it's for kids too, otherwise kids and teens aren't as interested.

Whatever...

Do you think I'm a teenager?

No, I call you rookie!

What do you think I am?

I'm not the one who thinks.

Big surprise there. Alana responded to her second voice sarcastically but she had one more question for it.

Why do you say all of this stuff?

I only live to stir things up in your life and I do know that occasionally you need some advice of your own.

You aren't really alive, only to Jackie, Barbara and me!

We'll see. You know perfectly well what I mean, even if you did win second prize at playing my game.

"Are you and your thoughts done arguing with each other?" Jackie interrupted, apparently knowing what was going on inside Alana's head. She seemed to know that Alana's thoughts were almost two different people. They were like a split personality inside one head and heart. Occasionally it gave them all a good scare or a good laugh.

"My thoughts received this wisenheimer trait from Dad. It's no longer the sweet part of me."

That's weisenheimress to you!

You, shoo!

"She said she prefers weisenheimress," Alana said out loud to no one in particular.

"You possess a very peculiar intellect," sighed Barbara.

"I actually like being different. It's better than being a popular zombie, like on TV."

"Alana has an overly large imagination. I have an average mind, and you have a smart mind," Jackie said to Barbara.

"You do have an eye for fashion and you really know how to decorate, so you also have a stylish mind." Alana looked at the outfit Jackie wore. It was a bejeweled light pink tee shirt, sparkly blue jeans with a jean jacket and a matching pink bandana.

"I don't play," she teased. "I get some really useful tips from my cool Aunt Eve. She knows everything about big designers because she works for one. She literally knows everything there is to know in the fashion industry and how to be physically fit."

"Why don't you get some tips from your aunt that we can use for the school newspaper? This computer seems to be taking forever, but at least hearing news like that is makes me have more patience."

"Your computer isn't always this slow."

"Perhaps the disc drive isn't functioning properly." Barbara bent down and flipped a switch and pressed a button on the disc drive. There was a broken floppy disc (consisting of Mr. Shannonson's past, useless work) inside the drive. A power switch to the monitor had also been shut off. Alana and Jackie were amazed.

"Are you psychic or something or do you just know a lot about home computers?" Jackie asked.

"My uncle Steven, taught me how to adjust effects in the control rooms. He also taught me everything about computers. Defective floppy discs are known to have negative effects on a computer. They disrupt the boot-up process. Also the monitor should've been on."

The computer started working properly again and Alana was able to read her email. Just as the girls had predicted, there was a message from Jane in Alana's inbox along with a profile on Helligant, *The Planettes*, and Himcules from a website. Jane' email read,

> *I'm sorry that I couldn't call. I wanted to spend the rest of the time I had with my parents because I wouldn't ever see them together again. Thanks so much for making me feel better. I don't feel so lonely now that I know there are people out in the world who do care and I will always carry that with me. I think I know how to be better than I was.*
>
> *Love,*
> *☺ Jane ☺*

Alana felt like crying. After hearing news that awful, who could blame anyone for being depressed? Alana now fully understood why Jane was always difficult. She looked over at Jackie and Barbara. Another idea came to her. Alana was finally able to solve both of the two most darkest, difficult mysteries she had ever faced. It finally all became crystal clear!

Solved Like a Math Question

Dear Alana,

My friend is obsessed with her favorite celebrity, Himcules. She even scored a class in mythology so she'd understand better. I don't know what she sees in him, but I'd like her to cool down. -Icicle

Dear Icicle,

Everyone gets obsessed with celebrities but they are only people too. You should tell her what you think and could she not mention it every time in every conversation. She will get over it in no time. -Alana ☺

"That's it! That's the mystery! It so clear now can't you see?"

"Alana what are you talking about? Please give some more details." Barbara stood completely perplexed. Jackie felt she had only half of a clue. Neither one of them had the answer figured out. They weren't entirely sure what Alana was talking about. Jackie looked at Barbara who shrugged.

"Remember when Helligant played for a Cow Daze episode? I knew they had sung it differently than on the CD. I finally realized what was different."

"Yes, I felt it was different too, but I'm not a expert on punk music bands so I wasn't really sure," Barbara nodded.

"You kept saying that there definitely was a difference."

"I already read the band's profiles and what it says about Helligant." Alana clicked on the Helligant profile which read,

Helligant. *Organized in 2005 by Charlene Scarlette-lead singer,*

Jesse Spider-base guitar, Karla Weller- electric guitar, and Mark Barrs-drums

How it all began!
We all know Helligant. They weren't an overnight success. Read the following interview about how they became the successful crew they are now.

By Reporter, Emily K. Hatch

Charlene: Mark, Jesse and I met when we were nine and were in foster care. We ran away to escape when we had enough of all the hatred we received and were taken in by a loving family from a local town.

Jesse: We always loved punk music. At age ten we taught ourselves how to play from listening to our favorite band at the time, *Musick*. We met Karla at school because she had the same music class as we did.

Mark: She always loved to play with us, When the four of us finally got good enough which was around age fifteen, we formed a band. Our first gig was at our school talent show for which we wrote *Gravitation Zero*.

Karla: Once a talent scout came to town, we jumped at our chance. We almost didn't get our first record deal because we were competing for the spot against another band, but then the second band became too busy for the record company so we got the audition.

Charlene: We wrote a few songs about our life and made a demo CD.

Mark: The company really liked the CD demo and said that our group needed a name to complete it.

Jesse: I remembered in about our eighth grade year at middle school, this girlie gang was dissing our band by saying that we were elegance from hell. I suggested that their insult should become a name by combining what they said and turned it into "Helligant." So we became Helligant and the producers said the name fit our band theme. Charlene, Mark, Jesse and I put it to a vote and Helligant won by a landslide. It was either that or Mutating Mystery. Much to our surprise, we were successful, which was something that we never expected to be. Jesse, Karla and Mark couldn't believe it when we were scheduled to play out-of-town for the first time. The crowd enjoyed every song,

Mark: The others and I promised and tried hard to never let it go to our heads. We never went overboard, but I do have to admit that even I acted bigheaded a few times when we were alone together. We hope to stay as a band for a long time before the audiences get tired of our music. If our fans are loyal which they are, we will have no problem.

Karla: Jesse always believed in the fans, and he's right.

Emily K. Hatch: Helligant, the audience is glad to hear from you. Every fan wants you to stay together forever. You are one band that still has goodwill, and you do what other bands have not been able to do— you let kids continue to daydream. If you want Helligant to remain together, listen to their songs on WON.com (World on Net), or check out the video bio at Helligant.com. Pump up the Popular Punk Pros.

Jackie and Barbara finished reading Emily Hatch's article. It still didn't give them a clue about what Alana said she had figured out.

"I still don't get it!" Jackie still had less than half a clue at this point.

"You leave me pondering," Barbara observed.

"I'll explain." Alana began to clarify the mystery. "The Cow Daze episode was when Misty ran away to where her parents and everyone else's were living. She needed to get away from the pressure she was under. She had a great time visiting once more. That's when Helligant sang Gravitation Zero. The song relates to when Charlene, Mark and Jesse lived in a foster care home and how excited the three were when they were taken in. That's how Misty felt in the show. Helligant (well, three fourths of the band) could relate to her mood and reaction. That's why they seemed to play with more rhythm and emotion. They could actually feel what was going on, unlike in a recording studio where they just sing the song and don't really sense anything no matter how hard they try. Can't you see how similar it is to Jane's case?"

Jackie, who finally got it, at that instant responded, "Wow, Sherlock, I suddenly see the connection. It's as clear as a window on Fifth Avenue."

"What time does the clock say?" asked Barbara. "I have to get home if it's later than 6:30 p.m."

"The computer says 6:15 and my digital watch says the same time."

"I should get back. At least we all finished our homework and solved a mystery at the same time." Alana caught on to Jackie's joke. Once again, Alana's thoughts started in.

I'm back!

Take an all-expense paid trip to my exciting memories like the one's when you weren't around!

Do you mean when you were little? You couldn't remember anything then.

Those lame jokes aren't tickling anyone's funny bone!

It's not a bone, it's a nerve.

Like the one you are getting on right now!

Exactly!

It's not that funny. Don't you get that?

Alana had to talk some more to make the voice quiet down. At one point, though, it actually sounded familiar, almost like a person she knew or once was friends with.

Great, now I'm going to be nagged about that too!

Alana waved good-bye to Barbara and Jackie. Mr. Shannonson told Alana to stay inside while he drove Jackie and Barbara to their homes.

"Because I don't want you and your friends being funnier than me," he teased.

"Because you know that we're better than you were at age thirteen," replied Alana.

The real reason was because Mr. Shannonson didn't want the girls to be out too late talking. He told Alana that she needed to check over her homework to be sure she didn't miss anything for a pop quiz the next day. Alana strode to the computer room and looked over her homework. She was positive that nothing was wrong. Alana packed up her things and put them in her backpack.

Barbara had been showing them how to be more organized. Now that Alana had the computer to herself until 10:00, she decided to surf the web. Her email account was still open. The screen shone brightly in the darkened room. Before shutting down her home computer Alana checked for extra email. Her inbox was empty except for one email. She saw the email address; it was from Sean. Alana opened the message,

> *Jane and I aren't together anymore. She became convinced that I liked you instead. She also said that you liked me also. If that's true please respond. If not I'd like to know. I'm glad I've known you for years. But for now I'd like to be single. I hope that's OK with you.*
>
> *Sean*
>
> *P.S. Jackie gave me your e-mail address after the newspaper meeting. Your column is getting really good. I hope you don't mind that.*

Alana couldn't be mad at Jane at that point. She was glad she had a true friend like Jackie. She responded to the message...

> *Jane is right. I do like you back. I don't mind being single for a while either. I am also glad we are friends.*
>
> *Alana*
>
> *P.S. Your column was a hit in the papers today. It was very popular compared to the comics.*

Plans for a Fabulous Friday

Dear Alana,

I love music a lot and I want to start my own band but nobody I know is willing to put their time into it and nobody I know can play an instrument. I want to be a rock star when I grow up but I have hit rock bottom at this moment. Do you have any tips? -Rocky

Dear Rocky,

You can place an ad in the school newspaper or perfect your own talent while you're searching for your band members. There are many people in your town, I'm sure, who can play an instrument and want to be in a band. Whatever you do don't give up. -Alana ☺

After school, when Alana had finished her homework, she still felt she had lots of energy and needed to be outside. She called Jane first, who surprisingly, was free that day.

"Would you like to come on a bike ride?" Alana asked. "We can ride all over town."

"Sounds great, I'll be over in a minute!"

"You should wear sneakers. There are a lot of hills around."

"One of the best hills is where Jackie lives near Huckleberry Road. It's so much fun to ride with the wind in your hair. I invited you because I don't get to see you as often."

The girls, who of course left a note for their parents, took their bikes and rode around for awhile. Alana showed Jane where the best berry bushes were, a place that the elementary schoolers visited often. In return Jane took Alana through a narrow path that looked like it hadn't been ridden on in years.

She remembered when she was only nine. Jane would come to this secret hideaway many times to put off doing chores. The girls laughed at that memory, while Alana carefully rode the narrow path with her bike. While she and Jane were riding through the area, Alana's little voice came back.

This is a new one, the forest, a place you will never be bored. Leaf soon and come back later.

Now make like a tree and leaf. What do you think of that?

Not bad for a beginner, rookie.

The conversation was suddenly interrupted.

"Alana, you have that faraway look in your eyes again, why?"

"It's nothing, really. Let's ride around some more." In her mind, Alana thought, *Leaf soon so you have life left to be bored.*

She wasn't sure if the voice got the message but she completely ignored any more thoughts that popped into her head unless they had to do with the bike ride.

"It's almost time to start heading back to my house," Alana stated as she looked at her watch. "We saved the best for last, time to ride up to the big hill near Jackie's house."

When the girls finally rode up to the top of the large hill, Alana felt she had lost her extra energy. She was panting heavily, but the view was worth it. Alana looked at Jane who looked down at the view of houses and backyards. Alana decided to ride down first.

Suddenly, the wind grew stronger. The sun was almost blinding and Alana couldn't figure out what happened at that moment because the next thing she knew she was just sitting on her bike, patiently waiting for Jane to make her move.

She looked like she felt the same way. The wind had altered both their hair as they pedaled up the paved hill towards Alana's house. Alana looked at her watch which said, 5 o'clock. What she didn't realize was that in a house, not too far away another girl was watching. The other girl was wondering to herself, *Why is Alana bike riding with Jane and why couldn't I come along also?*

Starting Something Newer

Dear Alana,

One of my friends really likes a certain guy she's known for years, and she's abandoning me, her best friend, so she can try and flirt with him. I wish her the best but I'd like her to pay me a little more attention at school. It's only on the bus that she even cares that I'm alive. -Loveless

Dear Loveless,

Your friend probably has a lot on her mind as she probably wants to snag her crush before it's too late. Trust me she will still care about you. I know she cares but is super busy. If you tell her that you'd like more attention, I'm sure she will hang out with you more. -Alana ☺

Alana tried to concentrate on the computer. She wanted to call somebody, but for some reason she also wanted to be alone. She saw her dad working on the computer in his room. After a while he signed off. With a sigh, Alana did the same. There was only one other possibility. Alana called and reached Jane at her house on the first try. They made plans to see the movie *Mystery Madness* later. Since they both were thirteen, Alana didn't need her parents to come along.

*   *   *

That afternoon, around 4 o'clock, Alana met up with Jane at the Upstaged Theater. The girls bought tickets and popcorn and took seats.

The movie was a mystery about a young male detective and his female partner who discover a murder at a wealthy man's house while on vacation. The wealthy man and his wife were both assassinated. The police were looking for both the culprit and an heir to the rich man's billion dollar fortune. The prime suspects were: the man's stubborn neighbor, his wife's self-absorbed mother, and the aloof company manager. There were also some background characters: the wealthy man's butler, the company secretary, and a car mechanic (when the detectives' car 'accidentally' broke down.) The detectives were then threatened with a nasty message after their offices were destroyed. They were shocked, but both detectives agreed to never quit seeking the killer.

"What determination that took," whispered Jane. Alana agreed. She noticed some sort of light near her but didn't bother to see what that was.

The detectives found a gun in the manager's office when the male detective disguised himself as journalist reporting on the crime. A lot of the evidence pointed to the manager, but the female detective thought that the aloof manager was only an accomplice. She conducted a lie detector test on him. They found a picture of him, his brother and sister who was really the stubborn neighbor and also the company secretary. The manager and neighbor were after a will too, so that they could destroy the original and forge a new one that would get them the billion dollars.

That's when the male detective noticed something odd on the back of his partner's neck. It was a tattoo of the combination for a safe in the wealthy man's home. The female detective was actually the heiress to her grandfather's billion dollars. It was a major shock for her because the female detective never knew any of her real family or how the tattoo ever got on her neck. She had it since she was a small child reared in a foster home.

The police arrived on the scene just in time as the self-absorbed mother was really on the protagonist side and she had called the police. The antagonists had claimed that they would get even as they were taken to jail. At the same time a mob of reporters were crowding the two detectives after the discovery of the heiress. The two agreed on donating some of the money to charity.

Mystery Madness ended and the lights in the theatre came back on.

"What did you think of that movie?" Alana asked Jane.

"I liked the old version better because it was more of a private eye tale. This one did have a great story line and awesome acting. It's almost as if they took it all from right out of a best-seller book."

"So what do you want to do now that the movie's over and we have a half hour on our hands and wrists?"

"Well, the mall is right next door and the rain has slowed to a steady drizzle. Would you like to go there?"

"Why not, but maybe we should stay here. I did tell my dad that we would be at the mall if there was extra time. Why not, what have I got to lose?"

"Anyway, the parking lot is at the mall anyway."

Jane and Alana raced to the mall next door. Since they had a little money left the two girls looked around the shops and had a snack at the food court. Alana suddenly heard a voice behind her.

"Hello, what are you doing here?" It was Jackie.

"Hey, Jackie," Alana responded. "I thought you were in the city. Would you like to join us?"

"Yes, please shop with us!" Jane added.

"I got back from the city a little bit early but apparently not early enough."

"What do you mean? You were busy, Barbara most likely was busy, but Jane was available today." Alana was puzzled by Jackie's response.

"You know perfectly well what I mean!" Jackie's voice was cold and firm. Alana saw that her fiery mood matched the cherry polka dotted shirt she wore. Jane looked at Alana with the same puzzled expression. Where was the little voice in her head when she needed it? She and Jane had no time to respond because Mr. Shannonson was waiting by the front door. They tried to wave good-bye but Jackie was already out of sight.

Confused in a Clique

Dear Alana,

My birthday is coming up and at school everyone knows we have a tradition of decorating lockers but nobody ever decorates mine. People only remember my birthday when I bring in some food. How will anyone ever acknowledge me instead of the things I bring in? -Always Forgotten

Dear Forgotten,

People are always stressed at the beginning and end of the year. So don't feel that they don't like you. Drop hints that you want your locker decorated and if nobody gets the hint, just decorate it yourself. -Alana ☺

Alana tried to call Jackie that night. She only reached Mrs. Donner. She tried to email her friend. She knew Jackie was always quick to respond when she was on the computer. Tonight nothing came up in her inbox. Her best chance was to talk at school the next day. Unfortunately there was less than a week left of the school year.

Alana didn't see Jackie at school either. She wasn't sure what she had done wrong. All she did was hang out with Jane a little more. Alana would try to do what she could to fix this problem. She finally caught Jackie at lunch sitting at a table near the bulletin board. Alana sat down next to her.

"Will you care to explain why you are so steamed?"

"Will you care to explain why *you* are forming a clique and lying?"

"Lying about what?"

"Lying about that you hate big cliques!"

"What the heck are you talking about? Of course I don't like big cliques because someone is always ignored. That's what happens all the time in class."

"That's what recently happened to me," Jackie replied angrily.

"Once again, I don't understand your meaning." Alana felt more puzzled than ever.

"Like you're losing a friend," said Jackie.

"Get to the point!"

"Well let's see.." Jackie pretended to think as she tapped her purple bandana. "You are forming a big clique and leaving me in the dust."

"OK, now you're being a drama queen!"

"Let me finish, you are making friends with enemies!"

"*Enemies*! Are you saying you don't trust Jane? Or are you just jealous?"

"You have some sort of clue."

"Jackie, come on, you know I could never exclude you." Alana realized what was happening. Her voice became softer as she continued to speak.

"I've known you for years and years, since we were five. That's longer than I've known anyone. Why are you jealous? I hang out with Barbara and nothing's wrong there."

"That's when we all are together! Yesterday, I tried calling you and your mom said you were at the movies, I saw you there with Jane and I couldn't stand it. You also looked my way and didn't care—one big clique-lover." Jackie's voice was still firm but the bitterness was gradually going out of it. "I was wearing glow-in-the-dark necklace charms."

So that's what it was! Alana thought.

Well it wasn't a shooting star, Rookie. Her other voice had time for a smart comment.

You keep out of this!

Alana said to Jackie, "Look, we've been a clique together for years, just the two of us. Can't we have other friends? Other cliques just keep their group the way it is and not open up to others. You know how other girls can be. Why do you think I've never liked the groups, no matter how kind the girls have been?"

"It was just fine before *she* showed up."

"Me thinks you don't want to accept her because you think it might jeopardize our friendship." Alana caught on to Jackie's thoughts.

"Me thinks she should keep away. Either she goes or I go."

Jackie really didn't want to be a clique with Jane. Maybe it's because she knows and understands what trouble cliquey groups are. Maybe she is taking the idea too far that these kinds of groups shouldn't be around, Alana thought. She tried to calm down Jackie as best as she could.

"Jackie, think about it, would you rather be in a clique with her as a change, enjoying the rest of our years at JWMS? Or would you rather have it the old way with insults, threatening notes, mean pranks, scared younger kids, and trying to survive James Walk like it was a jungle trek?"

"Let me think about that and I'll email you my answer."

That night when Alana checked her email she saw two letters. One was from Jackie and the other was from Sean. She opened Jackie's letter first. It read,

> *I may not care for being best friends with Jane but I'll accept her as best as I can. I would rather have school as heaven and not a jungle trek.*

Next Alana opened Sean's letter. It read,

> *I just emailed to say hi, this wasn't a dare.*

You Have a Lot, Including a Heart of Gold

Dear Alana,
*   I like this person in class. She is giving me hints that*
she likes me back and I want to ask her out. How do I make
the first move? -Saturday

Dear Saturday,
*   If you are ready to ask this girl out, do it before*
someone else does. She isn't going anywhere so you have
plenty of time. -Alana ☺

Alana loves Sean! Sean loves Alana!
The weisenheimer-ess was back at it again and this time
it 10:30 at night. Alana was too tired to come up with a
clever comeback so she merely moaned.

Be quiet let me sleep or I won't let you visit my new memo-
ries.

Nice come back, the voice droned sarcastically. *I'd like*
to be referred to as Wise Girl please.

On the up side to that, at least the voice had a name.
Alana never got that far with even a stuffed animal.

Fine, Fine, Fine! Just please let me sleep or you won't
even be a peep Wise Girl.

But I'll be around for when you and your lover boy chit-
chat.

Just shut your trap!

That finally got Wise Girl to quiet down and Alana could
finally sleep in peace.

*   *   *

The next morning at school, Alana met up with
Jackie. Alana knew Jackie would want all the details about

Sean. On the other hand, Alana wanted Jackie to keep the news on the D.L. (down low).

"I can't believe it. This is as amazing as Barbara's memory. Before I forget, I'm sorry for the drama-queen act."

"That's all right. But I don't want the other news to spread around, OK? Thanks for giving him my e-mail address."

"How did you..."

"Never mind that."

Holy psychic. The smirk in the teasing voice told Alana that Wise Girl was back.

You back from mine and Jackie's family's trip to Mexico two years ago?

Why do you think I called you psychic?

Look, Jackie and I have to go to class.

I'll keep a record and use it later for your pop quiz.

And you call me telepathic?

No, I call you psychic. Wise Girl brought up another point. Would she ever vanish once and for all? Alana decided if Wise Girl wouldn't vanish it was going to take a long time adjusting to her.

"Your split personality voice is back again?" Jackie was familiar with how Alana's imagination works.

"She prefers to be called Wise Girl now," Alana said. "Do these voices all disappear eventually?"

"Yes, although this one might stay longer than most, perhaps days, weeks, months or even years."

Got, that right.

You, stay put and take notes for the quiz.

"You are still speaking to me, right?" asked Jackie hopefully.

"Of course I am. Why wouldn't I? Don't worry I'll try to balance out everything. But don't, like, take any of my stressed out tones too seriously."

The girls sailed into Ms. Limner's class. There was a new student teacher at the front of the room. He had dark auburn hair, had a very young face, and wore a Red Sox pin. His name tag read, "Mr. Pikture."

He appeared to be around Ms. Limner's age. Wise Girl was on target again because there was this exam paper on her desk. The pink paper wasn't hard to spot in the mess of white and sculptures of puppies.

So did you study at all instead of goofing off?

Yes, I studied how to ignore you. Also I do pay attention and know the material well enough don't I? Remember nobody ever failed in Ms. Limner's class because she does a lot of extra explaining."

The student teacher handed out the quiz. It was the history final. Ms. Limner gets very creative for finals. She often told stories about when she taught at other schools. One of her former students was an eighth grader at James Walk. Today she was quiet. She looked around and pursed her lips slightly. Alana suspected she was interested in the new teacher. She didn't know much on love lives but it was a possibility. Alana looked at the first few questions on her history final.

Who was the greatest world conqueror in the ancient world?

Who first settled in Rome?

What was ancient Egyptian paper called, and what source did it come from?

Match four Greek gods with their Roman names.

Venus	*Herra*
Juno	*Aphrodite*
Neptune	*Ares*
Mars	*Poseidon*

Alana kept silent for the rest of class. She knew most of the answers, except for questions like,

What year was the beginning of the decline of the Roman Empire?

She wasn't very good at remembering dates in history so she took a guess from the multiple choice answers. She peeked at her watch, 10:45. There were only fifteen more minutes before French class and then lunch and free period. Alana saw that Jackie was already finished with her quiz. She only had one more question to answer.

When Alana finished she doodled on the back. Time seemed to scurry because the class had already packed up five minutes before the bell chimed. Alana pulled out her French binder and her vocabulary list. She knew that Miss Puxxle would plan a word search, just like Jackie's Latin teacher Mrs. Mapella often did. They both had to learn a little Spanish, so they took a course for the remaining semester.

In French class, Miss Puxxle added some bonus words to the list. The class had to guess the meaning's first. Alana called to Wise Girl for some advice. Alana understood she would dread that decision later.

Bonjour ma petite fille. Or do you need that translated also?

Since I need your help this time, I'll let that slide.

The three words Miss Puxxle wrote were *la semaine, une horloge,* and *Les ans.* Some of the other girls near Alana didn't have a clue about the words, but some did. Alana wasn't sure about some of the words, although since the unit was on "time," Alana tried her best to guess what the words meant. Wise Girl wasn't any help as she just kept playing a comedy routine (that Alana and her family were watching last night) inside Alana's head. So she knew she was on her own.

When Miss Puxxle told the class that they were allowed to use the dictionary all you could here were pages flipping in the classroom. Most now guessed the words correctly. When the class was over and Alana reached her house she found a letter on the kitchen table with no return address. She opened it, and noticed a scrawled note on a slightly large piece of paper which read,

I wanted to say this before the school year ends. You

have a lot of smarts, talents, and a heart of gold! Guess who! I love your jokes also.

Alana knew that the message wasn't a joke because she could tell that the writer's hand was shaking when it was written. That meant it took careful planning. The handwriting wasn't from a girl because it wasn't neat enough. That ruled out Jackie, Jane and Barbara. Guys at James Walk couldn't care less about their writing except one and he was the creative guy Alana knew and liked. Lucky Charms do have their golden confidence arm.

Wise Girl and Jackie Play Matchmaker

Dear Alana,

I am worried about my scores on the final. I normally get great grades, but I didn't study as well as I should have and I'm positive that the grades are lower. Am I over reacting? -Perfectionist

Dear Perfectionist,

Nobody is perfect. If you know you should have studied harder, it's too late to do anything. If you don't like your grades, than ask if you can do some extra credit to make up for it. The important thing is that you tried your best.
-Alana ☺

Jackie came over the next day. She saw the letter Alana left in her room. Wise Girl also popped up again like a poltergeist in a haunted house.

Miss me?

No! Do you prefer any other names besides Wise Girl?

I wouldn't mind being called the Fresh Princess of Bluewood.

Like that's ever going to happen. You and I are completely different; I like Cow Daze and The Planettes. *You prefer actors like Will Smith and things that have to do mainly with wisecracks and laughs.*

Mostly the book you forgot about when you stopped being the giggly girl I know and annoy!"

What do you mean? Of course I still joke around.

Not as much as you used to. I appeared this time because you completely lost your sense of humor. You are really losing your character.

What, that's impossible!

No it's certain, since you've had to focus on lover-boy Sean, your work, and your friends, you don't pay the slightest bit of attention to me, or the gags that we used to pull.

Alana remembered what Jackie said when she slept over weeks ago. She decided that she wouldn't mind having Wise Girl around after all.

Maybe you aren't all bad. Boy I'm going to miss you when you vanish into thin air.

That comment woke up my sleeping heart. I'm not going to stay, but I'll still joke around to be sure that you can still laugh and will stay that prankster just like your old man and yourself, kid. With that Wise Girl's voice drifted off.

"Alana, you've been giving me a blank look. What's Wise Girl saying now?" Jackie asked.

"That I've been losing my sense of humor. Is that true? Am I turning into a serious square billboard? Even better news is she's leaving for good. I'll never forget her stirring things up."

"Not with that comparison, but we don't joke around as much as we used to. I do miss laughing out of the blue and remembering the corny gags we'd tell each other. We were weirdos in elementary school, but many kids are. Remember how the guys would act?"

"Yeah I do." Alana had an image of small boys tying each others shoes together and sticking woodchips down each others shirts like idiots.

"In a way," Jackie continued "jokes and laughing haven't been your prime focus lately."

"Jackie, you've seen Barbara again haven't you?"

"That's not what I'm saying. I'm merely saying that none of us in seventh grade have been ourselves due to the fact that it's the end of the school year and there is a lot of pressure because of the finals. Remember all the events occurred in the past few weeks? You're also not yourself because Sean is finally talking notice of you. In addition, Jane has become a whole new person and Wise Girl is always appearing and disappearing. You and I are becoming different people, even if we are still good friends."

"Look, today I don't want to be around anyone else except my best friend."

"Do you really mean that?"

"Of course, I promised you we'd be good friends forever. I'm really not known for breaking promises."

With that, Alana closed her eyes and remembered everything from the time when Ms. Limner announced their history final until what she was doing at this very moment. Some events didn't seem to fit in with what happened recently, like paying attention to what the mean girls were saying. As she was remembering, Alana noted that the Walk Street Journal was purchased more often now than at the beginning of the year. The advice column she gave was gradually improving. She saw that Sean noticed her more at school, and in addition, Jackie's column in the paper was also becoming a success. Even Ms. Limner's long hair was starting to get red again and all of Alana's classes seemed to be more lively. There was only about a week left of school and finals were taking place.

"Jackie, I'm really going to miss seventh grade. I see what you mean when you explained everything. You are playing matchmaker for me with the past and another side of me, the daring funny side. Maybe that's what created Wise Girl, and almost every unique event that happened. I finally figured I've been giving advice all along."

"Of course you have. Since you helped Captain Arben and Chris, I knew you'd figure it one day because your brain should be large enough to spot something like that."

"Indeed it is and it should be large enough. If yours is, mine is."

"You are so full of it!" Jackie replied as she rolled her eyes. Alana recognized and understood every single word she said.

The Final Chapter

Dear Alana,
*   I know it's a dorky thing to say but I know I'll miss school. I loved many things that happened over the year. Will I ever get over it? -Attached*

Dear Attached,
*   You will love many things in the next year coming. It will be full of great memories. The answer to your question is in your hands. -Alana* ☺

After the school finals ended for everyone, there were still many new events that somehow wiggled in to fill the remaining chunk of the school year. Alana and Jackie taught Barbara some jokes so she'd come out of her shell a little more. There was some great news when Barbara announced that she was skipping seventh grade and they'd all be in classes together. They celebrated with the stars of Cow Daze at Steven Charles' studio and *The Planettes* played a song for them all after their newspaper meeting while Mr. Shannonson and everyone at the studio had the day off.

Jane's family reunited at a family picnic. She began to make many new friends at school. As a result Jane she resigned from the school newspaper committee to spend more time with her family and her new girl friends. All the girls and even the guys in her class complemented her on her new natural look without all the make-up that she once wore.

Sean became the new editor-in-chief of the newspaper and improved the paper's articles by letting Jackie and Alana to work together on the advice column. They got rid of the advice name "Candy Apple" and simply renamed it "Alana's Advice with a Jackie Jubilee." Alana now signed off with a smiley face. The web page had a new look. The advice inbox received over ten e-mails a day, but obviously some were made up stories. Alana and Jackie expanded their column (with permission from the editor-in-chief) so they had a whole page full of the letters they answered together.

With the assistance of Wise Girl, Alana and Jackie always stayed happy and laughing and even used some of her one-liners to weave into their letters if it was occasionally called for. Alana saw that her advice during the year had an effect on at least two students. A seventh grade boy, Ian Russell and a girl, Ashley Tanner who were both known to be shy, were seen talking together and even started hanging out more. Alana guessed that they were the ones who had sent their letters to the paper that one day. Jackie was getting known for her idea of decorating web pages as well as the school corridors. They lit up with life for the new school year.

Ms. Limner and Mr. Pikture had become very good friends and even started dating after about a month. Ms. Limner's hair turned red again because she had lightened up on her work. She gave five bonus points to all of her students, none of which got below a C on her final. Report cards were delivered to homerooms and Alana was pleased to see that she had gotten all A's and B's. Jackie and Barbara compared report cards with her and naturally, Jackie received a compliment that read, "full of life and style."

Barbara ended up getting the best grades out of the three, and she even exceeded her own personal expectations.

One of the compliments Alana received was, "full of laughter and knows how to keep the class laughing."

"Not exactly what my goal was, but I'm fine with the grades." Alana told herself.

You should be proud of yourself, rookie.

Very funny, and of course I'm very glad.

Wise Girl finally vanished from Alana's head. She now appeared as a small imaginary body that sat on Alana's shoulder. Jackie and Barbara could tell when Wise Girl appeared and disappeared. Wise Girl wouldn't come often but she helped Alana and Jackie when they were answering advice letters, sometimes sweet, sometimes wisecracking, and together they always left the many readers satisfied.

Alana, Jackie and Barbara agreed to sign up for the newspaper committee again when school started in the fall. They hoped that they would end up with the same homeroom teacher. However, there was only one little bit of sad news from James Walk. The principal, Mrs. Belling was retiring because she was going to have a baby sometime during the summer.

"Congratulations," was the word that every school member offered. Alana and Jackie made cards for Mrs. Belling before she left on the last day.

The Planettes even wrote and played a new smash hit single, due to their adventures called, Advice Girl, She's the One.

Advice Girl
She's the one,
She's the one
She's the one who knows her fun.
She's the girl who knows what's right
Despite
The fact she's had galaxy-sized troubles of her own
We know she is the person that we've always known

She's the one
She's the one
It's the girl who knows her stuff
Even when her life gets rough
She's the one
She's the one
We know the girl who gets it done
And that's why she is number one

Everyone knows it well enough
She always helps as best as she can
Even when she doesn't have her man
Due to the haters that usually have a plan
Our star never lets them get to her
Cause she is the only girl with the cure

She's the one
She's the one
It's the girl who knows her stuff
Even when her life gets rough
She's the one
She's the one
We know the girl who gets it done
And that's why she is number one

Advice Girl you take no trash from anyone
'Cause you're the star who'll get things done
We hope you reach where no earthling's gone
   before
Everything travels out the door
Impossible to happen to you
Hoping that you keep your cool

She's the one
She's the one
It's the girl who knows her stuff
Even when her life gets rough
She's the one
She's the one
We know the girl who gets it done
And that's why she is number one

She's the one
She's the one
It's the girl who knows her stuff
Even when her life gets rough
She's the one
She's the one
We know the girl who gets it done
And that's why she is number one

We know you're Advice Girl number one!

That was the sign that summer had truly begun. Every-one deserted the school and all that was left in the James Walk hallways were the lonely lockers.

Sean and Alana crossed paths again after school let out. By eighth grade they felt that seventh grade was the lucky year as they hung out one-on-one for the first time. "It's about time they ended up together," observed Jackie. "They've finally realized it. It took long enough."

Lovebirds, it figures. You never know what will happen next when they fly and flitter everywhere, responded Wise Girl.

During the summer, despite all she had been through that year, Alana felt that she was the same person she had always been. She offered advice, joked with her Dad, and felt she had to answer all the letters that came to her col-umn. She was true to herself. She made sure to always keep her lucky necklace safe. It had really come through for her, even when it was on vacation.